LITERACY TECHNIQUES

FOR BUILDING SUCCESSFUL READERS AND WRITERS

DAVID BOOTH

LARRY SWARTZ

2nd Edition

Pembroke Publishers Limited

KH

© 2004 Pembroke Publishers
538 Hood Road
Markham, Ontario, Canada L3R 3K9
www.pembrokepublishers.com

Distributed in the U.S. by Stenhouse Publishers
P.O. Box 11020
Portland, ME 04101
www.stenhouse.com

We acknowledge the financial support of the Government of Canada through the Book
Publishing Industry Development Program (BPIDP) for our publishing activities.

We acknowledge the Government of Ontario through the Ontario Media Development
Corporation's Ontario Book Initiative.

Library and Archives Canada Cataloguing in Publication

Booth, David
    Literacy techniques : building successful readers and
writers / David Booth, Larry Swartz. — 2nd ed.

Previous ed., edited by David Booth, published under title: Literacy
techniques for building successful readers and writers.
Includes index.
ISBN 1-55138-173-7

    1. Reading (Elementary) 2. English language—Composition
and exercises—Study and teaching (Elementary) I. Swartz, Larry.
II. Title. III. Title: Literacy techniques for building successful
readers and writers.

LB1573.B66 2004   372.4   C2004-902673-9

Editor: Kat Mototsune
Cover Design: John Zehethofer
Typesetting: Jay Tee Graphics Ltd.

Printed and bound in Canada
9 8 7 6 5 4 3 2 1

8/16/06

Contents

The first edition of *Literacy Techniques for Building Successful Readers and Writers* was a collaborative effort of over sixty new teachers. Thanks to the following teachers and writers for their contribution to this remarkable book.

Ann-Marie Adams
Diana Attar
John Bairos
Helen Belcev
Melanie Brennan
Maria Bruno
Lisa Bunga
Drue Burnstein
Suzanne Ceccato
Eric Chercover
Costa Cristou
Graziella DeLorenzi
Georgia Demakopoulos
Kimberley Erickson
Maxwell Evans
Silvana Febbraro

Frank Galati
Jerry Georgiadis
Shannon Grant
Andrew Hall
Andrea Hastick
Leeanne Hoover
Robert Kay
Waheeda Khan
Sarah Kurita
Sherman Lam
Zita Lapinskas
Loreen Lee
Michael Lee
Martin Lewis
Anria Loubser
John MacMillan

Michele Martin
Kimberley McCallum
Morgan McQuay
Wendy Menzcel
Julie Millan
Vivian Milios
Kally Nastos
Avy Ouaknine
Marilyn Orszulik
William Parsons
Mary Piercey
Deanna Pikkov
Tammy Pochmurski
Wanda Postill
Lilian Pritchard
Rosa Puopolo

Elissa Rodriques
Paula Rosa
Karin Schemeit
Chan Seow
Caroline Simmons
Kathleen Simon Lee
Claire Slater
Walter Teres
Christina Tolone
Efthimia Tsianos
Reinaldo Valverde
Andrea Van Kampen
Denise Westbrook
Melanie Wolfe
Jimmy Yee

Preface: The New Literacies

Since literacy is now defined as more than words on a page, the exploration of "the media" — computers, television, film, magazines, and so on — has been seen as an integral part of the learning continuum. Students of all ages need opportunities to be critical viewers to ensure that they become media literate. We have to consider the effect of these media and their influence on the thinking, reading, and writing proficiencies of children as we develop school curriculum. Viewing — the observing process — is an essential component of communication. The technology of the future will bring an ever-increasing flow of visual information that students will need to learn to comprehend, analyze, and apply to new situations. The critical strategies we hope to develop in students as they interact with print are just as necessary to their interaction with television, film, and the computer screen, or technologies yet unknown and undeveloped. Therefore, listening and viewing are vital elements in any literacy program.

Our students are not learning to be literate the way we did or even the generation before us did. Their texts have video, animation, hot spots; in their world, the written word has been extended by the visual and the tactile. What we need to ask ourselves is, "What kind of dispositions do our children need as they enter school today?" What is clear from looking at modern communication is that the visual landscape has dramatically changed over the past two decades.

In a digital environment, the new literacies involve thinking, exploring, connecting, and making meaning, often collaboratively. Students have the amazing potential to take advantage of vast global networks, huge databases, immense archives, rich art collections, and interactions with millions of users. Our task as educators is to help young people become capable navigators of what is often a complex and disparate landscape.

The inquiry-based classroom supports the development of a full range of literacies, as students handle the unexpected and the unfamiliar as well as the predicted and the known. Our students must create answers rather than collect them. In an environment filled with opportunities for reading, writing, and discussing, students create their own rich web of related questions that help them organize and structure their investigations and develop their emerging understandings.

Technology, in and of itself, does not necessarily improve the acquisition of literacy. It requires the careful crafting of learning programs focused on creating dynamic opportunities for the interpretation, manipulation, and creation of ideas in the classroom.

We need to help students skim and scan enormous amount of information, to select and organize what may be useful or significant, to critically examine the information for authenticity and bias. Teachers working with students who are struggling with literacy skills realize that a student's limitation with print texts often extends to the use of Internet information. Literacy needs remain constant with the different media experiences.

Current research supporting the use of computers in the classroom has been overwhelmingly optimistic. Many students find the computer a liberating approach to writing, and they often develop a more positive approach to learning. The development of a sense of purpose, understanding the connections between their work and the real world, a willingness to rework ideas and drafts, sharing with peers, using higher-level thinking skills, and developing more complex problem-solving abilities are all areas of growth for the students.

One of the great appeals of computers for students is that they are intrinsically motivating, and give students a great deal of autonomy in their investigations. For many students who have a natural predilection for solitary, fact-based activities, word processing on the computer is a natural and comfortable tool for learning. Of course, we need to move them beyond this rudimentary use of the technology to higher-order thinking — collaborating and creating opportunities that technology makes possible. We need to be aware that computer use may affect development in areas that boys should and need to cultivate, such as collaborative learning and the meta-awareness of texts they read. We need to help students to be active and critical in their use of multimedia, and vigilant that they do not get lost in cyberspace or incorporate inaccurate or incorrect information into their written work.

When the focus is on using technology to learn rather than concentrating on learning about technology, there are clear and connected language outcomes for students:

- Technology can help students be more productive and creative by providing access to engaging ways of representing ideas verbally and graphically.
- Technology can help students collaborate to publish, interact with, and use a wide range of media and formats to communicate information and ideas.
- Technology can help students research more effectively, using tools to locate, evaluate, and collect information. Technology also facilitates the processing, reporting, and presenting of conclusions and insights from data.
- Technology can help students work with others, including peers and telementors (online advisors), to solve problems and make informed decisions.

We are also aware of potential drawbacks in using the Internet, and must help students see that information on the Web is frequently inaccurate and at times incorrect.

- The adage "Buyer beware" can be borrowed here to become "Reader beware." Anyone can post a website on the Internet and, as a result, information is not checked for accuracy. Encourage students to use websites from established institutions and businesses.
- We need to monitor students as they use the Internet to ensure that they are where they should be.
- Not all search engines are created equal. As well, some students will be able to maneuver in any environment, while others will search in vain for information. Proficient peers can act as tutors to classmates who have less experience finding information on the Internet.
- We need to limit students' time on the Internet, given the demand for use by other students. Wandering the Internet, while entertaining, can be extremely time-consuming.

Part A: Supporting Literacy Learners

1. Conditions for Literacy
2. Parents as Partners
3. Creating a Literacy Environment
4. Twenty Ways to Support ESL Students

1. Conditions for Literacy

1. Reading is a meaning-making and meaning-driven activity. A reader requires prior knowledge to construct meaning with a text.

2. Reading success can be determined by the following: the context of the print; the format of the text; the style of the writer; the purpose of the text; and, especially, the background and life experience of the reader.

3. Writing is a complex act, a symbolic system – a means of representing thoughts, concepts, and feelings – that involves memory and the ordering of symbols to communicate ideas and feelings to others.

4. A child's attitude or disposition to reading and writing may determine his or her success in each act of reading and writing.

5. Individual aspects of writing (spelling, sentence structure, punctuation, format) are important parts of the whole process of writing, and can be focused on and learned through a variety of strategies that remain connected to making meaning with print.

6. While reading is much more than pronouncing words on a page, reading text aloud can be a significant part of becoming a reader and writer. Joining in the act of reading with one's own voice while others listen or participate leads to the satisfaction associated with belonging to "the literacy club."

7. The context in which a reader finds himself or herself may determine the nature of the literacy event. Reading a science report to a group differs greatly from chanting a big book with the whole community; a teacher listening with interest differs greatly from an outside observer conducting an assessment.

8. Each child's response to a text will be unique for a variety of reasons: social experience, cultural connections, personal interpretations of words and expressions, relationships with others, and appreciation of the author's message. We must support ESL students and incorporate their first-language literacy skills.

9. Members of a community of readers talk about personal interpretations and questions related to common themes that, in turn, affect the thoughts of others in the community.

10. Reading and writing are closely connected processes of learning. A student who writes down his or her thoughts thinks and reads while composing, revising, rereading, and editing the final product.

11. Literacy learning is developmental. Children proceed at individual rates, and teachers must provide the conditions that allow and enable their literacy learning to continue to take place. Teachers must have high expectations for each student's success, and support development and learning with appropriate and supportive attention that embraces the student's interests and needs.

12. Teachers need to read to students throughout the day, at times rereading the same text, and provide time for students to read. It is important to develop the students' familiarity with a great variety of texts and to have them reread passages and texts for authentic reasons to develop fluency.

13. Teachers may select books that share a common element: author, form or structure, theme, time, topic, setting, or contrasting views. Such structuring enables the reader to develop a perspective and an increased awareness of literacy resources.

14. For the purpose of developing the student's awareness of the scope of responses available to a text, the teacher should model particular responses.

15. Encouraging a student's personal response remains a priority. The student's individuality of expression and interpretation is supplemented by the guidance, encouragement, and knowledge of the enabling teacher.

16. Strategies for assessing a student's literacy growth can be introduced and developed in a variety of ways to sustain the interest of the student, increase comprehension, and generate variety in written expression.

17. Building word power in students is integral to their literacy growth. Teachers need to create opportunities for focusing on phonics instruction through games and activities using words from texts students are reading, as well as increasing sight-word recognition. Instruction in techniques for spelling is vital for their development as writers.

2. Parents as Partners

Children learn best when home and school literacy environments work together in partnership. Greater parental involvement in education may be the strongest single factor that promotes a child's success in school. Teachers can help parents recognize the importance of a child's literacy development in a variety of ways. When the school environment is seen as inviting, collaborative, and in need of their support, parents often become involved.

When parents continue to provide relevant information regarding their child's development, teachers have a greater potential for meeting his or her needs. Parents can encourage their children to build on the work they are doing at school, play a part in developing curriculum, and help as advocates for their children's school.

Parents need to be involved in the development of literacy. At the beginning of the school year, teachers can meet with the parents as a group to discuss their plans and goals for the upcoming year. During the school year, parental involvement and feedback about literacy programs can offer teachers a view as to what parents find most effective for their children.

Parent Volunteers

Supportive parents often serve as volunteers. Encourage male role models to participate whenever possible, since they, too, are essential for young children's literacy growth. Parents can

- listen to children read individually
- type children's stories so they can be published

Dear Parent or Guardian,

You are your child's greatest learning resource. Recognizing this, our school has developed a Parents as Partners in Learning program. Projects within this program encourage learning and reading at home. They also provide an opportunity for me to talk with you about your child's learning throughout the school year.

Classroom Lending Library
Your child can borrow classroom books on a regular basis. This is a simple and efficient system that encourages reading at home. It also helps your son or daughter to develop a sense of responsibility.

Book Bags
Each Friday, your child will receive a tote bag that contains four or five quality children's books that share a similar theme. The bag will also contain a list of the books in the bag, a letter to you, instructions, activity ideas, and materials your son or daughter will need to respond to the readings (e.g., puppets). Instructions for these book bags will vary from week to week.

Monthly Parent Bag
Each month, your child can select ten books to explore with you. The books, chosen by your child, can cover a range of topics and can include novels, non-fiction books, poetry books, and anthologies.

Newsletters, Dialogue Journals, Parent–Teacher Meetings
These give us a place to talk about your child's learning. Newsletters will supply information on school and class events, and general news. Dialogue journals will be of a more personal nature and will keep you informed of your child's school experiences. Parent–teacher meetings will be held periodically through the year so that we can discuss your child and his or her school program.

Your support of this program is greatly appreciated. Please feel free to call me at any time to discuss your child's learning.

Yours truly,

- help children do simple research
- read to individuals or small groups
- read stories on tape for the listening centre
- share personal stories
- work with children on projects and newsletters
- help children select books at the library

Connecting Home and School

Learning at home provides an opportunity for a parent, child, and teacher to work cooperatively. Some ideas that cultivate literacy at home:

Borrow-a-Book: Children choose a book to borrow from school and share it with a parent – reading parts aloud, retelling what was read, discussing it, and writing about it.

Share-a-Tape: Children use a tape recorder at home to interview parents, grandparents, and other family members telling stories. They share the stories by using the tape, a transcription, or an oral retelling of the story.

Recognize the Efforts of Parents

A monthly newsletter or calendar can include stories about the school's sports teams, upcoming arts events, after-school programs, etc. These can be written by children, parents, and staff. This format enables parents to act as literacy role models for their children while becoming informed about school.

Parent letters can be an efficient means of recognizing parental contributions to their child's literacy while keeping them abreast of class and school events. The following letter was written to parents when one school undertook a home literacy campaign.

3. Creating a Literacy Environment

Meaning-making with print can expand exponentially over time if we have wise others to support us. The landscape of our minds is constantly shifting as we read and reflect on what we have read, and our comprehension alters as we consider the ideas and opinions of others. We know that non-readers, unmotivated readers, reluctant readers, and limited readers can all grow with the right set of conditions. Those who work with adult illiterates tell how their students eventually, and with support, come to be print powerful. Youngsters in remedial reading classes can make great strides with guidance and instruction. And those who struggle with reading – some of them teachers and professional writers – with the help of someone who understands the literacy process can gain membership in what Frank Smith called "the literacy club."

When youngsters develop strategies for understanding different texts, monitoring their own reading, and writing their responses, they are on their way to becoming fluent, independent readers and writers who can assume control and responsibility for their learning. Along the way, they need secure environments in which they can experience plenty of success in their literacy ventures, where they feel safe to experiment and make mistakes on their way to learning. Teachers can often identify the children who are read to regularly at home as having an educational advantage over those who have not had similar experiences, adding weight to the argument that strong literacy events should be part of a child's life beginning in the infant years.

Students need many opportunities to preview books, notice words on screens, take part in literary events, and talk about books in order to enter the world of reading. They must see themselves as successful readers and writers from the beginning, and teachers must demonstrate a full range of reading and writing strategies in order to build their confidence. When children see a reason to read and write, most will want to become literate. The creation of real-life reading and writing situations, developing from specific needs in order to accomplish goals, results not only in literacy but also in pleasure, satisfaction, and a lifelong understanding of the reading and writing processes.

Environmental Print

Most children begin to notice how print works long before they start school. Children first learn to read from the print that surrounds their daily lives (including television and computers) and through repeatedly talking about and listening to the predictable patterns found in favorite stories and songs.

Some of the first words children recognize will be found on labels, signs, and menus. We do not need to teach these words, as children automatically attach meaning and relevance to them and their symbols. In a literacy-based classroom, the environment is full of print: signs, books, magazines, computers, stories, labels, and lists.

Variety of Materials

Students' reading and writing environments can include a variety of materials that will allow them to pursue interests and discover new information while developing their literacy skills. Classrooms, libraries, and home environments can offer abundant resources that are appealing and relevant to children, such as books, magazines, newspapers, computers, and other reference materials. Writing materials – pens, markers, pencils, paper, keyboards – provide a palette and canvas for children's written expression. The integration of technological aids – computers, word processors – helps children develop skills that are important to their future, and the use of these tools acts as a motivator for further reading and writing.

It is also important to have a large quantity of reading material available to students. The years between eight and thirteen are considered to be the "quantity" years, in which children gain reading power through in-depth experiences with a profusion of reading materials, including biographies, science books, and novels. Often children of this age will enjoy reading several books by a favorite author, or a series of books with a familiar set of characters. However, a reader's taste may shift frequently. Moreover, a vast supply of books is necessary to satisfy the range of reading levels within a classroom. In addition to providing books for new learners, students who have become independent readers need to be challenged with materials that present problems and situations of greater complexity, contain subtle characterizations, and provide contexts that challenge their concepts and ideas.

Surround Children with Print

Literacy development is a seemingly natural act that requires an unnatural environment. Effective classrooms are those that surround children with print; displays of text demonstrate to children the power of writing and may foster and shape their natural desire to express themselves. Students need a way into the world of words. They need to hear, talk about, read, reread, write, explore, and experiment with print to develop and internalize literacy strategies. Effective teachers surround the students with an environment full of interactive print experiences with printed texts of all kinds.

4. Twenty Ways to Support ESL Students

1. Take time for personal contact with ESL learners at least once during every lesson.
2. Avoid emphasizing correctness, as this may inhibit communication. Accept that mistakes are part of the language-learning process, and encourage students to continue talking. Involve language learners in engaging group tasks and problem-solving activities that promote interaction among the students.
3. Communicate a positive attitude toward second-language learners. Students who are learning English are not experiencing language difficulties; they are becoming linguistically enriched.
4. Use material and plan activities that feature repeated language patterns; e.g., songs, chants, games, picture books.
5. Instead of teaching parts of speech and other language concepts by first teaching a rule or definition, provide examples from which learners can figure out a rule or pattern.
6. Take a long-term view. Learners need hundreds, perhaps thousands, of opportunities to hear, read, and use target grammatical structures, as well as supportive feedback, before they fully internalize English language forms.
7. Introduce newcomers as speakers of their first language and point out that they are learning English.
8. Ease the integration of newcomers into the classroom:
   • Learn how to pronounce the students' names.
   • If possible, seat beginning learners of English beside someone who speaks it as a first language.

- Provide same-language partners for newcomers.
- Photograph every student in the class for a classroom display. Encourage students to write a mini-biography to accompany photos – some may produce bilingual autobiographies; some bios may be written in a student's own language.
- Organize structured group interviews to help students introduce themselves to one another.
- Create and distribute a language survey. Students can administer the survey with a partner or respond to it privately in a journal.
- Trace students' roots on a world map that is permanently displayed in the classroom.
- Invite students to interview each other about how, when, and why their parents or ancestors immigrated.

9. Classroom exhibits should reflect the lives and work of the students, as well as their contributions:
   - Include material in languages other than English.
   - Change displays regularly.
   - Involve students in creating displays.
10. Organize a peer-tutoring program, assigning specific tasks to peer tutors and partners.
11. Collaborate with staff in nearby schools to link elementary children with adolescents who can act as mentors, tutors, and role models.
12. Provide demonstrations to help English-speaking students understand how they can actively help students who are learning English; e.g., repeating or rephrasing, using gestures, transcribing words, seeking clarification, confirming comprehension.
13. Learn simple expressions in students' languages. Encourage students to learn words and phrases in one another's languages.
14. Provide multilingual reading material in school and classroom libraries.
    - Involve parents and other community members to help find material in their languages.
15. Organize multicultural literature circles that integrate varying cultural perspectives into the curriculum and help students develop a problem-solving approach to racism and other forms of equity.
    - To validate cultural diversity and broaden students' cultural literacy, select a variety of books that deal with a particular theme in various cultural contexts.
16. Help students become familiar with the rhythms and intonation patterns of English:
    - Read aloud often.
    - Encourage students to listen to books on tape while following along in a printed text.
    - Choose language-arts software that allows students to click on specific terms to hear how words are pronounced.
    - Lead students in choral readings of phrases and sentences to help them produce correct stress and intonation patterns.
    - When introducing new words during a lesson, always include pronunciation practice. Say the word, articulating clearly, and write it on the chalkboard or chart. Then, say it again.
17. When teaching grammar structures:
    - Teach and practise them in contexts in which it is natural or necessary to use the structure repeatedly.
    - Avoid introducing new grammar structures unless they are appropriate to a student's current level of development.
    - Highlight a specific language feature rather than attempting to deal with all students' grammar errors and problems at once.
18. Encourage students to guess the meaning of new words, using context, illustrations, and other cues.
19. Involve students in role playing, focusing on the use of expressions for a specific function.
20. Second language learners must learn to use specific communication strategies when communication is difficult. These strategies include
    - paraphrasing to confirm comprehension
    - seeking clarification
    - finding an alternative way to express an idea
    - substituting an all-purpose word – such as "things" or "stuff" – for an unknown word in the target language
    - asking for help
    - repeating with rising intonation
    - guessing at the meaning of a word based on the context or by analogy with other known words
    - using nonverbal signals
    - approximation
    - creating a word following a known pattern

(Adapted from Coelho 2003.)

Part B: What's in a Word

5. Learning Words

Children need to play with words. Through exploring, constructing, and talking about words, they begin to develop an awareness of how words work. Readers need to learn how words work so that they can read with fluency and meaning.

Encountering Words in Text

- By seeing difficult or unfamiliar words in a variety of texts, students apply their knowledge of word decoding to make meaning from unknown words. The more children read, the more familiar the words become, and the more efficient is their subsequent recognition of those words. They begin to see themselves as effective readers.
- A bank of sight words or familiar vocabulary is necessary to make sense of a particular piece of text. When there are too many unfamiliar words to decode, a student loses control over the context. Since sight words are necessary for progress in reading, teaching strategies that promote automaticity of word recognition is vital for developing readers.
- Children gain new print words through extensive reading and follow-up discussion to ensure that the words become integrated into their personal discourse. Teaching lists of new words out of context has little or no potential for increasing vocabulary.
- Teachers can teach strategies for inferring the meaning of words best through the context of the selection (and seldom through direct instruction). Students can use texts that are memorable (such as rhymes and rhythms), those that follow predictable patterns, and series like "Toad and Frog" in which the same words are repeated. They can, as well, read their own compositions and teacher-generated texts that highlight or repeat core words.

Making Words Their Own

- Students need to develop a sense of ownership of words they are learning to recognize. They recognize and retain words that are meaningful to them, and need to use components of known words.
- In order for a word to enter a child's personal vocabulary, he or she needs to generalize its meaning and apply it to a new authentic context. Students can increase their word power by using words in the context of authentic language events – meaningful talk, real reading and writing. They gain new vocabulary from their experiences with language used in context for real reasons – books, television, games, talking with friends, and overhearing parents.
- Students will choose from their reading those words they make part of their own vocabulary. Readers can often substitute words meaningfully and continue to understand what they are reading. They can return to an unfamiliar word as meaning accrues through their contextual understanding.
- Students can examine a text during a demonstration lesson and point out words that the author has chosen because of qualities the words possess and predict meanings as they connect new words to their personal, internalized lists.

6. Alphabet Activities

Research makes it clear that readers and writers require alphabet knowledge. Alphabet centres for young children should include a variety of writing instruments: pencils, pens, magnetic letters, alphabet books, and a computer, if possible. At the centre, children can experiment with writing – they can trace letters, draw letters as art, make rhyming word cards, construct words with the magnetic letters. etc. As children's knowledge of the alphabet builds, so does their awareness of corresponding sounds.

1. "Twinkle, Twinkle Little Star "

Countless numbers of children have learned to sing the alphabet to this age-old tune. Those children who know the verse can teach their classmates the song. To help them, you can point to each letter of the alphabet as it is "sung." An incidental moment for learning can occur when children line up to leave the class. Randomly assign each child a letter – they can order themselves according to the alphabet.

2. Sharing Alphabet Books

There are hundreds of books structured around the alphabet that can be read to and by children as they become aware of the twenty-six letters. These books can tell stories, celebrate individual letters, portray riddles, and add joy to learning the alphabet. You can use alphabet books at every age and stage of reading; the alphabet is an amazing structure for writers.

3. An Illustrated Alphabet

As a whole-class activity, make an illustrated alphabet. The alphabet can be themed, such as fairy-tale pictures, or it can be a mixture of images. Students draw one or two images for each letter of the alphabet. Work with the students to ensure that the words they choose to illustrate do not begin with consonant blends. Instead, brainstorm for other words that also begin with that letter but provide a pure sound (e.g., *cat* vs. *chair*). Display their completed work at children's eye level for easy reference.

4. "Grandmother Went to Market"

Students form a large circle. Ask one child to begin by saying, "Grandmother went to market and asked for an apple." The second child repeats this and adds another word that starts with the letter "a." When children can no longer remember all the items, begin with "b"; continue down the alphabet.

5. Letter Detectives

Provide students with magnifying glasses to search for letters around the room.

6. Eye Spy

Use frames without lenses or silly sunglasses and play the I Spy game, looking for letters displayed in words throughout the room.

7. Letter Sorting

Select a handful of plastic letters for students to examine. Invite them to find letters with straight lines, curved lines, tails, etc.

8. Highlighting

Go on a letter hunt using magazines or newspapers. Provide students with highlighter markers and invite them to highlight specific letters.

9. Animal Alliteration

Provide the students with a stuffed animal or doll. Children can suggest alliterative names for the toy (e.g. Billy Bear). Invite them to name things that this animal might like that begin with the same letter; e.g., Billy Bear likes burgers. He eats them with buns. His favorite colors are blue, black, and brown.

10. Survey

Each child writes the first letter of his or her first name on a sticky note. Notes are displayed on the wall or the board to form an alphabet graph. Which letter is the most popular? Which letters are missing?

7. Phonics

Phonics is a part of the process of word recognition, in which readers use their knowledge of how words work to make sense of an unfamiliar word. Phonic understanding must grow from what a reader knows about how words work.

Phonics Instruction

Young children sometimes think phonics drill sheets represent reading, and that sounding out letters is all that readers do. Instead, they need to understand, through a teacher's demonstrations, that word games and phonic instruction help them to focus on words while they continue to read, unlock letter patterns, and decode to make meaning.

While teachers need to teach phonics through repeated demonstrations, mini-lessons, and conferences, it should always be done with the goal of helping children discover and construct words, stressing that they can successfully learn to make meaning with print, to read. Phonic instruction should help children to notice letter patterns that occur in a word or a family of words, stressing the larger segments in words as well as onsets and rhymes.

Students can begin by reading a story, then move to an analysis of unfamiliar or patterned words in the story, constructing generalizations about sound–symbol relationships from words in context. To read a word, it is helpful to see it in context to determine its pronunciation. Words can be isolated out of context as long as they grow from the context of a story or book, so that children can apply their new sound–letter knowledge.

Readers start with familiar words to unlock parts of unfamiliar words. They can then discover generalizations about sound–letter relationships, rather than being told them. By observing the students' needs through authentic reading and writing activities, teachers can help them develop skills of word recognition.

As students spell words the way they hear them, teachers can note their experimentation with sound–letter relationships and analyze their application of word knowledge. When students use invented spelling to write, they are putting their phonic knowledge into action. From these attempts, teachers can readily see their developmental level and where they may benefit from directed teaching.

Students often arrive at phonic awareness in the following order:

1. beginning consonants
2. final consonants
3. consonant digraphs (sh, th, wh, ch)
4. medial consonants
5. consonant blends
6. long vowels
7. short vowels

Long Words

Efficient readers, on meeting a long, unfamiliar word, tend to break it into recognizable chunks. They look for compound words, prefixes and suffixes, and familiar word clusters. Context then confirms the word recognition strategies they have used. Children learning to read require demonstrations and individual conferences that model these strategies.

Onset and Rime

Onset refers to consonants that precede the first vowel in single-syllable words, while rime refers to the letters that follow the first vowel. In the word *cat*, for example, the letter *c* is the onset; the letters *at* are the rime. While we all know that sound patterns in English can be inconsistent, there are some common patterns in the language. Knowledge of rimes, particularly in the early grades, can help children read and reinforces the importance of word knowledge – parts (e.g., digraphs, blends, vowel sounds), role (e.g., noun, verb), and meaning – in becoming a fluent reader and writer.

Phonemic Awareness

Many children find phonemic awareness (hearing the different sounds in a word) more difficult than phonic awareness (matching print to sounds). Barring physical challenges that limit auditory discrimination, we can help students to become aware of phonemics through

- read-aloud experiences – reading nursery rhymes and pattern books that contain simple pattern structures, and texts that support phonemic awareness
- exploration of pairs of words that share the same sound, then extending the activity to have students name similar pairs of words

Having students name sounds that are the same focuses their attention on sound units within a word. Rhymes, of course, share similar sounds – children can name rhyming words and make up nonsense rhymes containing one or more pairs of rhyming words.

---

8. Focusing on Phonics

Games and activities can promote an awareness of phonics, because the satisfaction of playing with words to gain knowledge is an authentic purpose for learning.

Sorting Words According to Length

On a series of index cards, write words of between two and ten letters. Explain to students that you will call out a number, beginning with "2." All students who have words that contain two letters come up and place their words under the number, which you record on the chalkboard. Continue until all students have placed their cards. Discuss with them why you didn't start with "1," and ask them to name all the words they know that contain only one letter. Together, identify the smallest and largest words, and the number with the most words under it.

Clap Syllables

Have the students form a circle. Ask one to step forward and clap the beats (syllables) in his or her name. Model the activity several times before asking the children to join you. Begin with names that have one syllable, building up to names that have two syllables, then three syllables. Extend the activity by asking students to clap the beats in the words that name objects in the room. Can they point to an object and tell you the number of beats in its name? When finished, write examples of single-syllable and multi-syllable objects. Clap the beats in each word and discuss with the children that longer words usually have more beats than shorter words.

Nursery Rhymes

Once students are familiar with a few nursery rhymes, break the class into two groups. The first group starts a rhyme, but leaves out the last word; the second group shouts out the word to fill in the blank. Other activities include:

- making up new verses to rhymes using the names of children in the class
- choral reading of rhyming books
- identifying words from rhymes that sound the same and writing them on the board

Little Words

Tongue twisters are a fun way to review consonants. Find one or two simple twisters and repeat them with the students until they can say them on their own. Make a poster of the tongue twisters, underlining the first letter of each word. Add a new poster for each tongue twister you introduce, and encourage students to decorate them.

Word Families

Begin by discussing with students the concept that word families contain words that have the same vowel ending and that rhyme. On a piece of chart paper, write *cat* on one side; *will* on the other. Students record the words in the same manner on a piece of paper. Next, write *hat* under *cat*; *hill* under *will*. Have students repeat and chant the words. Ask them to give rhyming words and record them in the appropriate column. They can chant the words in each list.

9. Sight Words

To read effectively, a reader has to recognize words quickly, accurately, and easily. Readers translate written symbols that are grouped into words into their oral representation, hearing them inside the head during silent reading. In order to focus on making meaning with the text, the reader has to become efficient at word recognition with as little effort as possible. Familiar words need to be recognized automatically; difficult words need to be recognized using a variety of techniques. Most of the words we learn to recognize almost subconsciously are learned as we read, where the context drives the reader toward making sense of the words if she or he is involved in authentic reading and construction activities.

Lists of basic sight words are useful because they tell us which words in our language are used most frequently. You can make your own list of instant words, using lists such as those shown here and on pages 116 to 117, and from words you observe your students writing frequently.

The First Hundred Instant Words				Words from 100–200			
Words 1–25	Words 26–50	Words 51–75	Words 76–100	Words 101–125	Words 126–150	Words 151–175	Words 176–200
the	or	will	number	over	say	set	try
of	one	up	no	new	great	put	kind
and	had	other	way	sound	where	end	hand
a	by	about	could	take	help	does	picture
to	word	out	people	only	through	another	again
in	but	many	my	little	much	well	change
is	not	then	than	work	before	large	off
you	what	them	first	know	line	must	play
that	all	these	water	place	right	big	spell
it	were	so	been	year	too	even	air
he	wee	some	call	live	mean	suck	away
was	when	her	who	me	old	because	animal
for	your	would	oil	back	any	turn	house
on	can	make	its	give	same	here	point
are	said	like	now	most	tell	why	page
as	there	him	find	very	boy	ask	letter
with	use	into	long	after	follow	went	mother
his	an	time	down	thing	came	men	answer
they	each	has	day	our	want	read	found
I	which	look	did	just	show	need	study
at	she	two	get	name	also	land	still
be	so	more	come	good	around	different	learn
this	how	write	made	sentence	form	home	should
have	their	go	may	man	three	us	Canada
from	if	see	part	think	small	move	work
Common suffixes: -s, -ing, -ed, -er; -ly, -est				Common suffixes: -s, -ing, -ed, -er; -ly, -est			

For a reproducible version of this chart, see page 117.

10. Word Walls

A word wall — a visual display of words children have learned — acts as an immediate, accessible class dictionary and aids in the assimilation of high-frequency words. Word walls should always be used to associate meaning and practise activities: frequently used words should ultimately be automatic, and not phonetically spelled, so that children can spend their time and energy decoding and understanding less frequently used words.

1. Five words per week can be added to a classroom word wall, usually on Monday, so that the wall will comprise 200 to 220 words by the end of the year.

2. Words can be displayed alone, with a picture–sentence clue, or with a picture–sentence poster displayed in the room.

3. Words selected for a wall are those students commonly misspell, confuse with other words, or need in their reading and writing.

4. Words are arranged alphabetically on different colored pieces of construction paper.

5. In addition to adding new words to the wall, children can read and write these words each day. Other word wall activities include
   - adding endings (e.g., -s, -ing, -ed) to words
   - handwriting
   - making sentences using the first letter and cloze to select a word that makes the most sense
   - making sentences from wall words

- mind reading: the teacher thinks of a word and gives the class five clues to guess the word
- ruler tapping: the teacher calls out a word and then taps out some of the letters without saying them or finishing the word – the students finish spelling the word aloud
- sorting words based on features (e.g., all words starting with "t," words that end with "b").

6. Word walls for older students can include words related to current events or topics they are studying in other courses. In this context, word walls can resemble webs, as words relating to shared topics are linked.

Classification Suggestions for Word Walls

- double letters (e.g., daddy, mommy)
- letter clusters (e.g., tion, ish)
- compound words (e.g., goldfish, housecoat)
- unusual letter clusters (e.g., aardvark, vacuum)
- prefixes (e.g., in, de)
- suffixes (e.g., -tion)
- root words
- two-, three-, eight-, and twelve-letter words
- silent letters (e.g., ghost, knock)
- rhyming words (e.g., hear, fear, near)
- homophones
- plurals – regular and irregular
- contractions
- abbreviations
- synonyms
- functions
- joining words (e.g., and, but, however)
- alphabetical order
- words that
  - have the same letters
  - begin/end with the same letter
  - rhyme
  - have the same vowel sound
  - describe the same theme or topic
  - have the same number of syllables
  - contain two root words
  - share a pattern: consonant or vowel in the initial, medial, or final position
  - contain smaller words in order
  - contain silent words in order
  - contain silent letters
  - share the same root
  - contain letters that can make other words e.g., sit – its)
  - begin or end with the same sound, but don't contain the same letters.

---

11. Word Banks

Word banks give children ownership and investment in the words they learn, increasing their interest and enthusiasm for learning in general. Students choose key words from their reading, based on a quality (e.g., sound, length), record the words on index cards, and file them in a personal word bank. Because the students own their banks, they recognize their words more easily. The teacher may add complementary words to the bank to emphasize concepts (e.g., sound–letter relationships), but it is the students who ultimately control their banks and the words in them.

Each student may have two sections in the word bank: one for words that are being learned, and one for recognized words. Words can be

- practised
- matched
- used in posters
- made into cartoon captions
- discussed
- sorted
- played with
- cut and pasted
- expanded
- used to generate rhyming words, phrases, or sentences
- shared
- traded.

Through the use of word banks, meaning is made as words are recognized effortlessly and used in both contextualized and decontextualized settings. The growing number of recognized words (50 to 150) enables students to independently read texts of increased complexity, as well as to write their own stories with confidence.

12. Word-Solving Strategies

Word-study activities generally take place before or after the reading of the text. Before reading, we introduce key words and concepts, drawing attention to language concepts and special, necessary vocabulary. During reading, we guide each student to apply increasingly flexible word-solving strategies in negotiating unfamiliar words. After reading, we review and reinforce application of strategies, and introduce new letter patterns and structures.

Our main goal for word study is to provide students with strategies for independence. Fountas and Pinnell (1998) refer to the process of figuring out unfamiliar words as "word solving" because it involves a variety of strategies beyond simply decoding.

Teach word-solving strategies one at a time, modeling them and providing opportunities for guided practice. Some teachers like to maintain classroom charts to remind students of strategies they should be using. Or you can create Strategy Bookmarks:

1. Choose three to five strategies you have studied and want the students to focus on.
2. Draw pictures representing these strategies onto slips of paper.
3. Laminate these bookmarks for the students to use as placemarkers and strategy reminders.

Top Ten Tips for Word Solving

1. Checking: Check the picture to help you figure out the word.
2. Chunking: See if you recognize any "chunks" or patterns. Is there a little word inside a big word?
3. Cross-Checking: Use word walls and other classroom charts as a reference for solving words in texts.
4. Stretching: Stretch the sounds in the word; sound it out.
5. Sliding: Take a running start and slide right into the word.
6. Monitoring: Stop and think about whether the word makes sense, sounds right, and matches the print.
7. Skipping: Skip a hard word and read on; sometimes the rest of the sentence will help you with the word.
8. Rereading: Go back to the beginning of the sentence and start again.
9. Fixing: If you read a word that doesn't make sense, sound right, or look right, go back and fix it up.
10. Guessing: Guess what word might make sense in the sentence. See if the sounds in your guess match the letters on the page.

Part C: Meaning-Making with Texts

13. Comprehension Strategies

Teachers want to help children develop into independent, purposeful readers who think carefully about what they have read. Often, readers in trouble make little sense of what they have been reading, or they choose to ignore meaning-making completely and give up in frustration. All children need effective comprehension strategies to become independent readers and writers. Teachers will need to promote thoughtful interaction with the text being read, so that readers will be able to focus on relevant information, make sense of it, and integrate that learning with what they already know.

1. Real reading experiences motivate students to explore the ideas in print further because what is being read will be significant to the readers, enabling "deep-structure" meaning-making to occur.

2. Teachers need to help young people reveal their thoughts about what they have read so that they can begin to reveal, clarify, modify, revise, and extend their frames of reference. If they are afraid to share their understandings, or misunderstandings, how will they begin to grow as readers?

3. Each child must focus on making personally in becoming a thoughtful reader. Comprehension is about thinking and understanding, and is affected by each person's knowledge, experience, and purpose for reading a particular text. Proficient readers are aware of the strategies involved in making the most possible meaning with print; they make predictions, make inferences, see images in their minds, draw conclusions, and revise hypotheses about the text.

4. Proficient readers take risks. They learn to make educated guesses, predicting what the print will mean, rereading for clues that are missing, confirming or making alternate predictions. By caring about the reactions children have to what they are reading, teachers can encourage them to speculate about the text, consider its meanings, reread for clarification, and recognize difficult words through word solving and context clues.

5. The maxim says, "It takes two to read a book." By organizing book clubs, literature circles, and discussion groups, teachers can help students increase their understanding of a text. As members reveal their reflections about what they have read and interact with their group in exploring the text, everyone has opportunities to rethink and modify their personal understandings.

6. Teachers can encourage students to respond in a variety of modes to what they have read, thereby helping them to think about the text in personal and meaningful ways. These interpretations – through art or drama, verbal or written – can be shared to increase everyone's understanding of how text can be interpreted, appreciated, and valued in different ways.

7. Rereading or revisiting the text increases understanding. Teachers who use innovative strategies for having students interact again with the selection help them extend their knowledge of the text.

8. Teachers can help students evaluate their own efforts as readers with activities and frameworks that promote sharing and exploration, and that continue the inquiry process for learning.

14. Encouraging Comprehension Before Reading

Many things affect how a reader makes sense of a particular text: knowledge of the content of the selection from background experience; familiarity with the author's writing style or other similar books; and an understanding of the issues or the setting of the selection. When teachers spend time with students before their reading, especially with material that is unfamiliar or appears to be of little interest, then they will help ensure that the reading becomes a more meaningful and satisfactory experience. Teachers help students build and activate their background knowledge so that they can integrate the new print text with what they already know. Prereading activities can arouse students' curiosity and give them a purpose for reading. Teachers may teach vocabulary necessary to understanding the main idea, but only a few words, since students need to learn to identify words from context.

Tapping into Background Experience

Concrete experiences before reading can broaden children's background knowledge. The more we know about a topic, the greater our background experience, and the easier it is for us to connect to a topic. Children who have visited zoos, for example, may have more background knowledge about animals than those who have not had similar experiences. By sharing and discussing these experiences, a child's knowledge of concepts and related vocabulary is extended.

Teachers can help students expand their personal experiences by involving them in actual situations, such as going on field trips, taking nature walks, and engaging in hands-on activities and experiments. If this is not possible, students can be provided with experiences through videotapes, audio recordings, drama, and discussions. The reading experience can be personalized by building on the student's interest with a selection. Students' knowledge and interest can be furthered by sharing with them background information before they meet the story on their own.

Previewing and Predicting with Texts

1. Brainstorm as a group what issues and events might take place in the story.
2. Describe what might happen in the story, based on prior knowledge and past experiences.
3. Predict, from a summary or cover blurb, what might happen in the story.
4. Formulate questions about the story or selection to be read.
5. Engage in a thematic exploration of ideas related to the story: view films; listen to stories; share poems; interview speakers; read extracts, articles, or summaries; conduct surveys.
6. Conduct a discussion about ideas and issues related to the text to be read, and share personal views.

---

7. Model the importance of prediction in reading. You can read the first part of the selection and then discuss with students what is happening and what will likely happen. Special formats and print conventions can be explained.
8. Examine a few difficult words that will appear in the text and predict what they are and what importance they may hold for the selection.
9. Stress the importance of predicting by reading/viewing together as a group or class, and discussing the ideas that different readers bring to a text.
10. Invite students to predict a text's vocabulary, language style, structure, and content from its title, cover, table of contents, pictures, photographs, diagrams.
11. Ask questions: "What do you know?" "What do you want to find out?" Encourage students to formulate questions using guiding words – who, where, when, what, why, and how.
12. Have students consider previous experiences related to what they are about to read or view. Questions can focus and extend the student's thinking about a particular aspect related to the material at hand. The discussion itself may also generate new questions.

15. Teaching Predicting Techniques

Advertisements

1. Share with the students a book or movie advertisement. Ask questions such as, "What do you see?" "What do you think this book/movie is about?" "What kind of book/movie is this?" "Have you seen this phrase or picture before?" "Where?"
2. Read/view the first part of the material with students, then ask them to discuss what is happening, using the information they have read/viewed and what they already know to justify their responses and to predict what may follow. Read/view the next part and repeat the process. When finished, students can check for predictions that have been confirmed.

Short Stories

1. Divide a short story into three or four episodes. Title each episode and record it on a separate piece of paper. Copy and attach the three or four pages so that each student or pair of students has a booklet.
2. Ask them to read the title of each episode and draw a picture of what they think it is about. When finished, students can compare and discuss their picture sequences.
3. Read aloud the story to the class. How accurate were students' predictions? Discuss with them how the titles helped/didn't help them to predict.

New Texts

1. Before reading an unfamiliar non-fiction text, write its title on the board. Ask students to brainstorm sentences they think will be in the text. (An alternative is to have students brainstorm on their own or in pairs, and record their sentences before a class list is compiled.)
2. As a large group, classify the sentences and display them where all students can see them.
3. During and after reading, they can note how many of their predicted sentences were included in the text.

   A variation of this activity is to ask students to brainstorm words that will be in the text.

Grouping

1. Provide pairs of students with a series of pictures, words, sentences, or combinations of these related to, or from, a text.
2. Ask them to determine methods of grouping, classifying, and sequencing the elements.
3. Students can share their work with another pair. Together, the four pool their work and present it to the rest of the class.
4. Make a class list of organizational methods.

Brainstorm and Categorize Information

1. Before students begin to read specific text, ask "What do you already know about this topic?" Record all responses.

2. After they have finished brainstorming, ask students to categorize or classify the information to give it a logical structure.
3. Each student can then identify what they want to find out by writing one or two sentences.
4. At the end of reading, take a class poll to find the number of facts that were answered by the book.

Before- and After-Charts

This activity reminds students of what they already know and helps them link this to new information. It also clarifies the purpose of reading.

1. Before reading, ask students to list all they know about a topic to be studied.
2. After reading, they write all they have learned.
3. Students then find a partner with whom they compare lists, and write questions they still need answered. Together, they research the questions and write a short report that details their findings.

16. How Books Work

Children need to be immersed in books of all kinds in order to become readers and writers. As well, they need to receive demonstrations of how books are constructed and used, since books vary in purpose, audience, format, and organization, as well as in the publishing devices and designs they employ. The type of book may influence the language it uses and the way in which information is presented. This, in turn, will influence how the book will be read. Consider how dictionaries, novels, poetry anthologies, diaries, and picture books differ.

Through familiarity with types of books and discussion about what readers do with them, children develop an understanding of how different kinds of books can be used. Some books can be read from beginning to end; others will require the reader to

• scan a book for a particular item of information
• read part or all of a book to better understand a concept
• read part or all of a book to follow directions

- read only a portion of a book
- refer to a book over and over again.

Awareness of how books work, and an understanding of book and print conventions, can be developed through activities that help students explore the components of print.

1. What Is a Book?

Consider, as a class, the question "What is a book?" before developing a reference chart of types of books (e.g., poetry, picture, narrative). Give students opportunities to classify books according to the chart they have developed.

2. What We Find in a Book

Make available a variety of types of books for students to examine. They may come up with a list such as this:

- both pictures and text have meaning
- text is usually written from left to right
- text is usually written from top to bottom
- words are represented by a letter or a combination of letters
- there are two forms of letters – upper-case letters and lower-case letters
- words can be highlighted by writing in different graphic forms
- print can be presented in lists
- words can be used as labels
- words can be enclosed in speech or thought balloons
- punctuation illustrates how to read a text
- some words begin with capital letters, depending on their meaning or their position in a sentence
- different forms of writing have different print conventions.

3. Parts of a Book

As you use books in class, you can draw the students' attention to the parts of books and the names of these parts:

cover	copyright	preface
chapters	contents	epilogue
index	title page	dedication
glossary	spine	bibliography

A group of students can develop a large diagram and label the components.

4. What's in a Title?

The students can discuss the importance of a book's title. To facilitate this, display, compare, and discuss various titles and their effectiveness. Can they identify the importance of an effective title? Can readers rely on a title to tell them about a book?

- Students can use the title of a book and its front cover to make predictions about what the story will be about. Record their predictions on a chart and post it for easy reference. After reading, they compare what they have read with their earlier predictions.
- Students can read or listen to a non-fiction book, then create a web of information.
- Cover the title and author of a book and give it to a pair of students. After reading the book, they decide on an appropriate title. They share their suggestions and justify their choice of title with another pair of children before reading the original title.

17. Monitoring Comprehension During Reading

Teachers now recognize that many students need support while they are reading, not just after they have completed a passage. Many factors affect the understanding of a text or the ability to continue reading it: the context in which the children are reading (peer group pressure, the physical setting), the purpose of the reading (the kinds of interaction, subsequent assignments), and supportive assistance (discussing a complex format, clarifying an unfamiliar phrase).

Teachers can encourage comprehension during the reading through directed, guided reading activities with a small group, or with dialogue journals that are incorporated during the reading of a novel, revealing the reader's thinking processes for later discussion.

Proficient readers use reading strategies, to build meaning and comprehend text automatically and seamlessly, as they work in real reading situations. We need to support all students in becoming readers with these strategies for overcoming difficulties they encounter, instead of permitting pretending or them to give up on a text. Explicit instruction, mini-lessons, and demonstrations can clarify procedures for them and increase their abilities to work with texts proficiently.

What Good Readers Do

When effective readers engage with text, they activate their background knowledge

- attempt to anticipate the events in the text
- process print with fluency, using punctuation and phrasing
- maintain a consistent focus on constructing meaning
- monitor and repair comprehension throughout the reading process
- recognize a large number of words automatically
- solve unfamiliar words using a variety of strategies while reading for meaning
- connect text to self, text to text, and text to world
- recognize and prioritize important ideas
- have questions in mind before, during, and after the reading
- draw inferences during and after the reading
- summarize and synthesize information during and after reading
- pictures in the mind while reading
- to text in order to reexamine, modify, and extend meaning-making

---

18. Marking and Highlighting Text

Highlight markers are popular among some students. Unfortunately, many of these students have had little practice in recognizing what is important and color in the entire page. They have had little or no instruction in sifting ideas. Students can practise by using two colors of markers and highlighting every word: one color for what they understand and one color for puzzlements and confusions. In this way, they can begin to distinguish what they know from what

they don't understand. They can discuss possible strategies to clear up the difficulty.

Distributing copies of a short text allows students to mark or highlight the page, especially if the books normally used are school property. On their own copy, they can code what is happening as they read – noting questions and subsequent answers, connections they make as they read, inferences they determine, "aha!" moments – making visible their own thinking patterns as they read. In partners or small groups, students can compare strategies, clarify difficulties, and share insights.

Colored sticky notes can flag prior experiences, thoughts, queries, and reflections as we read, modeling a technique that many readers use in their reading lives. At the conclusion of the reading, these markers can be pasted on a page so that the reading/thinking processes can be seen as a whole, and each student's pattern can be analyzed: Where were the difficulties? Which words or terms caused trouble? What questions arose? What connections were made? What was the author trying to say? How did I solve the confusion? What do I think about the topic now? Students can begin to see how they go about constructing meaning, identifying confusions, and monitoring their own reading.

---

19. Making Connections

Our main goal as literacy teachers must be to help students build bridges between the ideas in the text and their own lives, helping them to access the prior knowledge that is relevant to meaning-making with the text, the information that the brain has retained and remembered, sometimes accompanied by emotional responses or visual images. When we help students enhance their reading by activating their own connections, we offer them a reading strategy for life.

All kinds of connections whiz through our minds as we read a text, and these can lead to fascinating explorations, but generally we want to model and support those that promote deeper insights into our understanding of what we have been reading. However, even leftover reminiscences and queries may prove to be powerful resources if recorded in response journals during the reading workshop, where they can be developed and extended into thoughtful writing events.

The connections have been classified as three types:

1. Life Connections: text to self – connecting to past experiences and background
2. Text Connections: text to text – connecting to other texts in our lives and to the forms those texts take
3. World Connections: text to world – connecting to events in the world at large

As the three general categories interconnect and intersect, students have a strategy for coming at a text selection in a variety of ways. As they begin to observe and reflect upon how these connections affect their understanding of a particular text, they can deliberately use each aspect of the connection frame to increase their personal and collective processes of meaning making.

Making Life Connections

Making connections needs to happen as we read, so that we are constantly expanding and processing different types of knowledge.

During a demonstration with a shared selection, we can list the connections that everyone is making on a chart, and then label them by type. At the conclusion of the mini-lesson, the students can select a specific connection and develop it in their writing notebooks.

Before the students begin to read, we can elicit what they already know about the topic or the theme of the book, and list their ideas on a mind-mapping web or a chart. Through guided discussion, we can prompt them to see that they do have connections to call upon that will support their reading – events from their own lives, bits of information gleaned from previous experiences with television or magazines, or stories they have heard from friends and relatives. The more prior knowledge we can tap into, the greater the meaning-making that will occur when we read.

We can show the students how to code their responses while reading by having them mark the text with sticky notes whenever they make a connection. These notes can form the basis for a discussion in which students articulate their connections and begin to notice how our reading

minds function. We need to help students understand how each connection relates to the text, and how it deepens or extends their understanding.

> Maxine Bone and Susan Schwartz have articulated their construct of connecting in their book *Retelling, Relating, Reflecting*. We might say as we work, for example,
>
> This reminds me of…
> I remember when…
> It makes me think of…
> It makes me feel that…
> That happened to me, too, when…

Making Text Connections

We can help students begin to recognize text connections by selecting particular text sets to be used during independent reading or literature circles: books related by common themes or writing styles; books about the same characters or events; several books by the same author or from a particular genre; different versions of the same story. Comparisons and contrasts offer us a simple means of noting text-to-text connections. As students see other relationships among texts, we can record these on a chart as a reminder to make connections as they read.

Often students remember and bring forward past text experiences to clarify or substantiate a present discussion. They reveal that they are using text-to-text connections for deeper learning, tying what they have met before to what they are presently exploring, and expanding their literacy perspectives. We can, of course, model this with our own comments during a class discussion.

By drawing attention to the features of different types of print texts, we can help our students understand how texts work, the nature of different genres, and the cues and literacy features of each. The more familiar they are with the characteristics of a text, the more accessible it will become, and the more easily they will be able to read it. They will know what to expect when they read a novel, a science text, a poem, or a letter; they will recognize the intent of a speech, an editorial, or an article; they will know how a particular author structures a novel and why a narrative can be told through letters.

Making World Connections

In our own work in the teaching of reading strategies, we are seldom satisfied unless the learning stretches outside the classroom lives of the students, connecting our reading to bigger world issues so that perspectives and assumptions are challenged or altered. We are grateful to Paulo Freire for giving us the expression "reading the word, reading the world." Somehow, when we read powerful, significant text, we travel outside ourselves, exploring what lies beyond our immediate neighborhood, extending our vision and encouraging our personal meaning-making.

20. Questioning the Text

We read because we are curious about what we will find; we keep reading because of the questions that continue to fill our reading minds. Of course, readers ask questions before they read, as they read, and when they are finished. As we become engaged with a text, questions keep popping up – questions that propel us to predict what will happen next, to challenge the author, to wonder about the context for what is happening, to fit the new information into our world picture. We try to rectify our confusion, filling in missing details, attempting to fit into a pattern all the bits and pieces that float around our sphere of meaning-making. We continue to read because the author has made us curious, and this constant self-questioning causes us to interact with the text, consciously and subconsciously. As we read on, our questions may change, and the answers we seek may lie outside the print.

The deeper and more complex the text, the more questions we bring forward as we try to make sense of it. The greater our interest in what we are reading, the more substantive our questions will be. Monitoring our reading means paying attention to those questions that arise as we read, as well as those that remain when we are finished.

We begin to make our connections to what we already know, wrinkling our brows at incongruities or seeming inconsistencies. We accept that our minds work in inquiry while we read and that the questions that remain after the reading can form the basis for our text talk, for exploring further research or for just pondering and wondering about the complex issues that the reading has conjured up.

Often our most limited readers ask themselves the fewest questions as they read, waiting for us to interrogate them when they have finished the disenfranchising ritual of the prescribed print offering. They have not learned that confusion is allowed as we read, that in fact authors count on it in order to build the dynamic that compels us to continue reading. And as students grow in their ability to self-question, their understanding of how authors think and of how meaning-makers work increases.

21. Making Inferences

We spend our life making inferences, noting all the signs that help us make sense of any experience: the face of the salesclerk displaying a product, weekend weather reports, the body language of the students we are teaching. As readers or viewers, we make inferences when we go beyond the literal meaning of the text – whether it is a film, a speech, or a book – and begin to examine the implied meanings, reading between the lines to hypothesize what the author intended, what he or she was really trying to say and why. When we read, our connections drive us to infer; we struggle to make sense of the text, looking into our minds to explain what isn't on the page, building theories that are more than just the words. We conjecture while we are reading; the information accrues; our ideas are modified, changed, or expanded as this new text enters the constructs in our brain. Inferencing allows us to activate our connections at deeper levels and to negotiate and wonder until further information confirms or expands our initial meaning-making ventures.

Predictions are inferences that are usually confirmed or altered, but most inferences are open-ended, unresolved, adding to the matrix of our connections. Often we need to dialogue with others to further explore these expanding thoughts and to become more adept at recognizing the need for digging deeply into the ideas of the text.

If you are working with a group or the whole class, ideas from one student will prompt others to hitch-hike into the discussion. By recording these examples of inferring on a chart, the students can see how the thought process works, and how we must confirm, revise, and alter our hypotheses as we read along in the selection and, of course, as we talk about the text and hear other opinions.

22. Visualizing the Text

When we read, we create pictures of what the print suggests, making movies in our heads. These images are personal, each one of us building a visual world unlike any other. Reading words causes us to see pictures, which is understandable, since words are only symbols, a code for capturing ideas and feelings.

A Checklist for Visualization

❏ I create pictures or films in my imagination as I read, noticing what characters look like, what they are wearing, where the action is taking place, etc.

❏ I visualize scenes or details not described, picturing what had happened to the characters before the story began.

❏ I picture myself in the book, meeting the characters and being part of the scene.

❏ I understand why the writer uses certain structures and conventions to present a point of view.

❏ I notice how the text is organized.

❏ I comment on the way the writer presents or withholds information.

❏ I am aware of the writer, in purpose and intention.

❏ I combine and connect ideas, and am able to formulate my own thinking.

❏ I notice the vocabulary, the style, the "wholeness" of the selection.

❏ I negotiate, agree with, or argue with the writer's ideas and opinions.

❏ I use images from my own experiences to help me create a picture of the text.

❏ I connect to the emotions and the senses described in the text.

❏ I role-play and enact scenes of the story as if I were in it.

❏ I often draw as I read, depicting visual images of what I see in my mind.

❏ I identify words and phrases in the text that help me see in my mind the characters, places, and events.

---

23. Summarizing the Text

In the old manuals, *summarizing* usually related to the post-reading process of recounting in a few words what happened in the text. It appeared to be a quick means of finding out what young readers had thought about what they had read. But, as a reading strategy that occurs during the act of reading as well as at the completion, it is valuable to share with students. Summarizing is an organizing and reorganizing strategy that allows us to categorize and classify the information we are gathering as readers, so that we can add it to our storehouse of knowledge and memory. We need to constantly connect the new information we garner from the text and to find a way of making sense of it, so that we can assimilate it into our ever-developing construct of knowledge. How would we ever remember the tons of data we receive as we read without systematically adding it or rejecting it in our schema of understanding?

We summarize constantly as we read, sorting out significant ideas, events, and other bits and pieces of information. If we are reading a long selection or a complex and difficult piece of writing, we need to pause and regroup every so often, coming to grips with a means of classifying the barrage of information we are receiving. We might make notes to help us connect and remember details so that we can focus on the big picture; we might check the table of contents to strengthen our awareness of where a section fits into the whole; we might reread the introduction to clarify the framework of the information we are meeting. What we do as effective readers is use the strategy of summarizing as we read, getting the gist of the text.

Students are often plot victims; they simply recount the sequence of incidents that occurred in a story. The art of the teacher is to move them beyond synopsizing to a fuller consideration of what they have read and thought about. In the past, book reports were often simplistic recountings of plot: "and then he…" "and then she…" We want thoughtful, mindful interpretations and reflections of what students have read. Demonstrate a better strategy by having students use a double-column approach in their reading journals, for summarizing and synthesizing in writing. For example, they could work with the novel they have just finished reading: on the left, they summarize what happens in the story; on the right, they note their personal responses. The final written product can be a blending of the two columns. This separation and then integration of the two processes may help students notice the differences between summarizing and synthesizing.

24. Reading Critically

Analysis and criticism are connected processes: before we give our opinions, we need to carefully analyze the many aspects of the writer's craft that went into the creating of the work. We have all been disappointed by a student's review – "I hate this book" or "I love this book" – that is unsupported by any analysis of the points that resulted in the opinion.

We can help developing readers gain a deeper understanding of the text they are reading by giving them techniques for considering its effectiveness. As they learn to analyze the particular aspects of a selection, they may come to both appreciate the writer's craft and better understand their own responses to the text. They can begin to step back from the initial experience, to reflect more clearly about its effect on them and how the author conveyed the ideas and the emotions embedded in it. We can help students discover the underlying organization, the elements that identify the genre, the format of the selection (including graphic support), and the overall effect of the work. These are opportunities for guiding readers into a deeper awareness of the text, the author's techniques, and their own developing responses. Critical reading relies on the readers employing all the strategies they know in order to come to thoughtful, carefully determined conclusions about the value of the author's work.

Analysis should be a component of every discussion, as students share their personal responses and connections, raise their concerns and questions, make inferences from the informa-

tion, and talk about different aspects of the content and the style. Readers can move toward a critical appreciation and understanding of the text, as group members analyze and synthesize the ideas and responses that build cumulatively throughout the session. Each member should feel wiser about the text after the discussion.

We want readers to carefully weigh evidence from a text in order to make a thoughtful decision regarding their own opinions, to combine textual information with their own background knowledge. They need to draw conclusions and apply logical thought to substantiate their interpretations. We want readers to make and to recognize informed opinions.

We want our students to work toward independence, to develop into lifelong readers who see books as friendly objects, who recognize the art of reading (as Louise Rosenblatt, authority on reader response, said) as the negotiation between the author and the reader. We must help students think carefully about the texts they read, to become aware of how literature works.

Increasing Fluency

Since children become fluent by reading, and since meaning-making is a cumulative process, they need to read much more than a few minutes a day to develop into literate human beings. In a print-rich classroom, children have opportunities to read a variety of books for different purposes: stories in anthologies (or readers), novels, curriculum materials, poems, plays, and references. As well, children benefit from reflecting on what they have read, listening to classmates' interpretations, raising their own questions about the text, retelling what they have read, reworking and reformatting ideas (necessitating a careful examination of the text and a thoughtful response to what the author was trying to say), examining the author's style and language choice, and reflecting on ways in which individual class members bring meaning to the printed page.

Part D: Responding to Texts

25. Reasons for Responding

A teacher can extend a student's response to the text through a variety of activities. Limited readers, in particular, need to see the richness of literature response, and to recognize that a story is only a beginning point for expanding ideas and increasing language strengths. As well, a good story provides a powerful context for looking at how words work. What students do after reading should relate directly to what they have read and to what they need or want to do.

- Teachers want to encourage students to engage in "grand conversations," to think and feel and respond to the issues, the characters, the events, and the language of the selection. The focus is on topics of interest to the participants, and everyone's opinions are valid when supported by the text. Teachers can encourage them to share their thoughts and experiences with their classmates, extending the meaning making for everyone.
- Teachers need to integrate the language processes by ensuring that response activities provide opportunities for further reading, writing, speaking, and listening for thoughtful reactions that further language growth. Students need to use language to articulate ideas and to interact with the thoughts and feelings of others.
- At-risk readers require group members who will listen to one another, who will help activate background knowledge and build upon it, each learning from the other as they share and contribute ideas. By using a variety of grouping patterns, teachers can offer each student flexible settings for growth, ensuring that the purpose will determine the groupings. Heterogeneous groups, whole-class and sometimes ability groups, offer students opportunities to grow in particular skills and to engage in discussion and activities with a variety of students who offer different strengths. For example, ESL students need to read, write, and talk in meaningful contexts in cooperative and collaborative settings that encourage interaction. They require a modeling of language by participants engaged in using English for authentic purposes.
- Literature instills a love of reading, but not when it is accompanied by fragmented activities. Instead, activities need to be integrated, significant, and thoughtful sets of response modes that encourage students to think about what they have read long after the book has been closed.
- The development of independent readers is best accomplished by an enabling adult through the purposeful structuring of literacy experiences. It remains valuable to read to students throughout the day, to reread the same texts, and to provide time for them to read. It is important for them to develop familiarity with a great variety of texts, to reread passages and texts for the sake of developing fluency, and to read selected parts of material in order to develop varied reading responses to the text. In providing structure, books may be selected that share a common element: author, structure, theme, time, setting. Included might be different versions of the same book or contrasting views. Such structuring enables the developing independent reader to build a perspective, and thus increases response to both the form and content.

Teaching Tips

1. Establish a core set of resources for the classroom:
   - sets of books to be shared (e.g., novels, anthologies, collections)
   - a collection of books for independent reading (e.g., novels, biographies)
   - curriculum resources (e.g., texts, kits, media).
2. In the beginning, you can use prepared resources (e.g., book guides, manuals, idea booklets) that accompany selections in anthologies or readers. These offer starting points for literature exploration, and free the teacher to observe and work with each child to personalize the activities.
3. Provide a variety of response modes from which children can select.
4. Model and demonstrate examples of various response strategies.
5. Share, display, and discuss reading responses with the class.
6. Display examples of effective responses from previous classes.
7. Organize a class chart or schedule of reading activities each week.
8. Design activities surrounding a specific author or illustrator.

9. Establish reading contracts and schedules for conferences and group activities.
10. Encourage and negotiate with children to undertake a variety of response activities.
11. Create folders of follow-up activities for each selection (e.g., question guides, author information booklets, documents, websites).
12. Make a reading response folder for each child. Students can record books read, those they want to read, and the time spent reading.

26. Talking About Books

The reading experiences of children can be extended by what other people reveal to them about their reading and what they reveal to others about their reading. Text-based discussions in the classroom give students the opportunity to construct meaning from the text by returning to it to clarify and support their ideas, ultimately directing their learning. Giving students the means to engage in discussion about a text gives them the power to edit and reform their perceptions, as well as to expand personal meaning and deepen comprehension.

Talking as a Community

- brainstorming ideas about concerns for discussion in small groups
- predicting and anticipating, and clarifying the story to be read or heard
- relating the story to other classroom concerns, such as thematic units, genre, or style
- building background about the story's setting, characters, concept structure
- allowing a forum for summarizing, bringing forth points of view
- sharing talk that happened during group interaction
- allowing for feedback and different interpretations
- giving opportunities for film and video versions of the story, and for authors and illustrators to lecture and demonstrate
- setting up occasions for panels, seminars, public speakers, interviews, debates

How to Get Children to Talk About Their Reading

To encourage talk, the teacher often asks questions. The art of teaching lies in those questions and in handling the responses they engender. If we list our questions, we should be influenced by students' questions as well, and therefore our personal list must never be seen as sequential or controlling, as a dull agenda to be covered. They are signposts for the journey, and may be welcomed as directions when the talk becomes disjointed or argumentative.

Perhaps the most useful opening is "Tell me about the story." This can begin the journey inside. The teacher must create a middle ground that allows students to learn about the story, balancing the response between their experiences of it – their thoughts, feelings, and observations during and after the story – and the content of the story itself – theme, plot, characters, and form.

In *Booktalk*, Aidan Chambers states that the art of reading lies in talking about what you have read. Like all readers, children want to discuss what they have enjoyed about a story. They want to explore those aspects of the story implicit in the text and ponder the connections they have made between the story and their own lives and the lives lived in other stories. He has provided a very useful chapter dealing with sample questions of an open-ended nature that have helped to provide lively interchanges of personal meanings among youngsters. Although we could create a long list of sample questions, Chambers once stated in a workshop that the following four questions would stimulate all the discussion you could hope to have:

- What parts did you like most?
- What parts didn't you like?
- Was there anything that puzzled you?
- Did you notice anything in the story or poem that made a pattern?

1. Letting Individuals Prepare for Discussion
Students need time to reflect on a text and to formulate their own ideas before they discuss them with others. Teachers can encourage them to record their responses to a text as a preparatory step to discussing them in peer and group situations. The act of recording a response may increase their comfort level at later stages.

2. Discussing with a Partner

Students can share their thoughts and ideas about a text with a partner. They can use their recorded responses from the previous step to support the discussion if they wish.

3. Discussing as Part of a Small Group

In small groups, students can discuss and reassess their original ideas and possibly modify their thinking.

4. Sharing as Part of a Large Group

Depending on the nature of the discussion, ideas stemming from small-group discussions can be shared among classmates. This form of sharing can be done by jigsaw grouping, whereby each child, in his or her small group, takes a number from one to four. Students from other groups who took the same number form a second group. New group members take turns sharing their previous group's discussion.

Talking About Text

1. Book Clubs

Have students meet on a regular basis (e.g., weekly, monthly) in groups to discuss books they have read. The book clubs can be organized according to various genres; for example, fiction, non-fiction, poetry, science fiction, and mystery.

2. Book Recommendations

Students take turns to recommend a book to the rest of the class or other classes in the school. A class poster can be created to display their recommendations and ratings. Students can decide and vote on rating categories.

3. A One-Minute Book Talk

Students can select a book they have read. In a one-minute time period, they share their opinion of the book in a small- or large-group situation.

4. Share Time

Provide a daily time for students to share thoughts about a book they have read with the rest of the class. Keep a record of sharing times in order to ensure that each student has an opportunity to share his or her reading at least once a week.

5. A 30-Second Radio Spot

Students can prepare and record a 30-second advertisement that recommends a book they have read and think others would enjoy. These advertisements can be prepared for other classes in the school, based on individual and class responses to books. Advertisements could be played over the public-address system.

6. Story Objects

Have students bring an object to class that represents the theme of a story they have read or heard. In groups, they take turns outlining the relevance of their object to the story.

27. Asking Questions that Matter

In past decades, students were often required to prove their mastery of curriculum content by answering teacher-generated questions, most of which demanded brief, factual responses. This method of teaching often encouraged them to memorize answers, but did little to foster in-depth inquiry, a necessary component of deep-structured learning.

As educators extended their understanding of how children learn, they modified their questioning techniques. They know that open-ended questions can serve a variety of functions:

- introducing reading tasks by stimulating interest and curiosity;
- setting up problems that require reading;
- identifying important ideas to look for when reading;
- reinforcing and organizing ideas gained from reading; and
- helping readers construct meaning by using questions that initiate dialogue.

How can we help youngsters to interact with the text as they read, to care about what they are reading and become engaged with the meaning-making that reading requires?

We can begin by showing how we ask questions ourselves throughout the reading experience, demonstrating the process and writing down the questions that come up in a selection we are sharing. This public monitoring of our reading can often help student readers recognize how interacting with text works, and it may even free some of them from their own restrictive patterns of regarding the text as a frozen maze that seems unsolvable.

If we introduce students to this inquiry-based mode of reading, they, too, can demonstrate their own self-questioning strategies. We can begin with a shared selection to read aloud, using copies or working with the overhead projector. Students can use sticky notes on their copies to note their questions as they read. After they have completed the text, we can categorize the questions according to type: .

1. questions that were answered as we read further
2. questions that can be answered through inferences as we make other connections
3. questions that simply cause us to wonder

Ways to Use Questions

• We can model and demonstrate how effective questions work, showing the need to listen carefully to others, revisiting points in the text that support a particular comment, and supporting effective responses of the students.

• Try asking no questions during a text discussion, but note down the ones you might have asked in the past. Or record a text talk session between you and the students, and play it back to analyze the types of questions you used and the effect on you students' contributions.

• Rather than initiating questions, build on the questions and comments of the students by offering open-ended responses after they speak, encouraging further contributions and helping to focus and deepen the dialogue.

• Consider using prompts rather than recall questions. When used in your interactions with students during group sessions and individual conferences, and in you responses to their reading and writing journals, these prompts can expand or deepen the offerings of the students, help them clarify or expand their thoughts, and nudge them into expressing their opinions and ideas. We have questions to ask and we need to ask them, but we want to teach our students to ask their own as well.

• Separate assessment questions from your text discussions. If you clearly state the purpose of the assessment activity, whether in practice

---

sessions or in a testing situation, it can help students understand the difference purposes of each and to learn how to handle both types of events.

Teachers ask questions that help students to develop higher-order thinking skills and require them to draw on personal knowledge and experience. They foster environments that are conducive to sharing ideas and opinions, realizing that the environment in which questions are asked is as important as the questions. For many teachers, a natural outgrowth of this approach is the development of student-generated questions as an integral part of the classroom climate.

Teachers now know that for true learning to occur, children need to be able to pose questions to themselves. When children ask questions about a story, they require a detailed knowledge of the text and need to have thought deeply about what they've read. The ability to pose questions has application in all areas of life, and has particular relevance to tasks such as problem solving.

28. Retelling

Retelling helps children construct meaning from a text. In preparation for retelling, they can revisit the text after an initial reading. This increased exposure to the text may clarify and confirm for children their initial perceptions. In other cases, it might lead children to discover that they need to modify or change these perceptions – perhaps they overlooked the importance of one element or failed to see a connection between points in the text. Once children are satisfied that they understand the text – that their perceptions are accurate – they are ready to retell what they have read to others.

Retelling allows students to explore the language of literacy and reinforces their oral communication skills as they interpret tales to create personal meaning. The urge to share through telling empowers exceptional students to overcome language barriers. Through retelling, students can travel the world to meet and understand other cultures. Its sources are many – nursery rhymes, riddles, chants, show and tell…

1. Participation Stories
Engage students in tales that invite participation through cumulative, sequential, and recurring patterns where they join in a chorus or a refrain.

2. Cooperative Retelling
Students can share a story and then retell it, staying close to the plot of the original story. When finished, they add twists to the retelling to create a new story. (They can unravel a ball of yarn with knots throughout it to indicate a new twist.)

3. Fortunately/Unfortunately
This activity is most effective with small, odd-numbered groups. The first person in the group begins a story with "fortunately," the next person adds on to the story beginning with "unfortunately," and so on until each child has contributed. They then repeat the story chorally and chart it for others to read.

4. Round-Robin Storytelling
Begin the activity by dividing the class into small groups and asking each person in a group to read the same story silently. When they have finished, number off the children in each group. On a prearranged signal, #1 from each group begins to retell until the signal sounds. The #2 students take over, then #3, and so on (in this way the story is retold with no one person responsible). Students can explore first-person narrations by retelling from various points of view: "Tell the story through ____'s eyes," or they can try multipart narration in which one narrator shapes the tale while others retell from their chosen point of view. Finally, students can get inside the story by exploring a challenging or magical part; for example, creating a chant or rhyme to "help" the characters out of difficulty.

5. Storytelling Chair
Storytelling chairs are special places for telling stories. Here students share what they've read or written, and tell of stories in progress.

6. Retelling a Story as Part of a Small Group
Students form groups of five or six members. Provide each group with a copy of the same story. Members read the story and then develop a retelling. Each group presents their retelling. When all groups have finished, students can comment on the retellings and decide why different versions were effective.

7. Retelling a Story as Part of a Large Group
Read the title of a text to students. Ask them to predict the genre of the text based on its title, as well as the type of writing (factual, narrative), and possible words and phrases that may be included in the text. List their predictions. Read the text to them, or have them read the text. Students can check for predictions you listed earlier. When all have finished, ask them to suggest how they can retell the text orally as a large group. Record their suggestions on the board before holding a class vote to decide on the method of retelling. Students retell the text and reread the original text before comparing the two. Discuss, as a large group, any details omitted or changed in the retelling and the reasons for these differences.

8. Retelling a Story to a Group
Find a story that is unfamiliar to the class and share it with one student. She or he prepares and presents a retelling of the story to the rest of the class. All students then read the story. When everyone has finished, they can discuss the content and accuracy of the retelling and how it helped when they had to read it on their own.

9. Retelling Favorite Stories
Ask each student to retell in writing his or her favorite story. (For those who prefer to express themselves through art, they can retell the story through illustrations.) Collect the stories and compile them to make a book of class favorites.

10. Story Mapping
Select a word representing the key concept of a text and write it on a large chart. Ask students to brainstorm all the words they can think of in relation to the key concept. In pairs, they categorize the words to form clusters or a map of words. They label each cluster before sharing their map with others.

11. Picture Retelling
Following the reading of a story, provide each student (or pairs of students) with a long strip of paper. Ask them to draw a series of pictures that retell the story, and to include captions, labels, and signs where possible. Picture retelling can be used

with a variety of texts, including nursery rhymes, biographies, poems, and chapter books. Students can compare their retellings with those completed by their classmates. Did they choose to illustrate the same events? If not, how did this affect the retelling?

12. Recorded Retellings

Provide students with a tape recorder. Ask them to read through a text one time and then tape their retelling of the text. Have them reread the text before listening to their retelling. How similar was their retelling to the original text? Ask them to explain any differences. Similarly, you can videotape some of the retellings and replay them so they can evaluate themselves.

29. Oral Reading

Oral reading brings the context and words of a selection to life. To read orally, students need opportunities to prepare, practise, and rehearse their reading. When they are comfortable with the text, they can participate in the oral reading of it.

The benefits of oral reading are numerous. It improves comprehension skills, strengthens reading abilities, and enhances interpretation skills. When used as a diagnostic tool with young readers, it allows teachers to assess pronunciation, fluency, and reading habits.

Oral reading should not be confused with round-robin reading, which involves one child reading, then another, and so on. This form of reading is usually fruitless, since it seldom improves reading skills and does not lead to a deeper understanding/interpretation of print. Round-robin reading may even decrease a child's understanding and appreciation of the story. A child may decode beautifully yet understand little.

Teachers can model purposeful oral reading by sharing enjoyable excerpts of a book, making stories personal for listeners, reading good stories each day, reading poetry and plays, and encouraging children to read only when there is a wanting and waiting audience (after an opportunity to rehearse, of course). Teachers can provide a variety of models in the classroom through the inclusion of radio plays, news broadcasts, poetry readings, taped stories, teacher/parent readings, video-tapes, and so on.

When students read aloud, the teacher has an opportunity to monitor reading progress by analyzing the miscues they make. Listeners need to listen for meaning rather than correct the reader and interfere with fluency. Sometimes only the reader will have a copy of the material; if those listening have copies, they can celebrate the selection together by reading chorally or creating a dialogue from the text. The teacher must resist correcting a student reading aloud until she or he has sufficient opportunity and information to self-correct through monitoring for understanding – students need to develop their own strategies for handling print. If help is necessary, the teacher can give feedback that assists the reader in self- correcting: "Did that make sense?" "What word looks like that?"

Oral Reading Events

1. Reading Together (Belonging)
· Choral readings (e.g., poems, rhythmic stories)
· Big-book stories, chart stories, and poems
· Chants (select rhymes, parts of stories suitable for chanting)
· Tongue twisters
· Singing (present song lyrics so all can follow)
· Line/word-a-child poems (different students read different lines and words)

2. Reading to Share an Enjoyable Passage or Information
· Personal writings
· Findings from research
· Instructions
· Schedule for the day, announcements

3. Reading to Recreate Dialogue or Dramatize Parts
· Scripts (read silently first)
· Dramatize poems
· Readers theatre (dramatizing narration from a novel or short story)
· Story theatre (interpreting dialogue and narration with action and movement using, for example, fables and legends)
· Plays (prepare and perform scripted plays)

- Action rhymes and poems (devise or follow actions to accompany favorite rhymes and poems)
- Action songs (select songs where actions can be devised)
- Read and act (one or more children read a story while a group acts out the actions)
- Sound-effects reading (create effects using music, voice, and percussion instruments)

4. Reading to Prove a Point or Verify an Answer
- Reading select sentences and phrases to support personal views and ideas
- Taking quotes and passages directly from a story

5. Reading to Go Deeply into Context and Share with a Friend
- Reading buddies

6. Reading Their Own Writing
- Class books
- Chart stories
- Jokes
- Stories
- Journals
- Plays

7. Reading Aloud to the Teacher (Assessment Strategy)

30. Recorded Books

Tapes, DVDs, and CDs provide an alternative way for children to experience repeated readings of favorite stories, songs, chants, and poems. Their low cost and simple operation make them an ideal resource for every classroom, and they can be considered both educational and entertaining. Many community libraries and bookstores carry a wide assortment of book tapes, DVDs, and CDs for people of all ages.

They may be stored in plastic bags with the accompanying text or multiple copies of the text. Teachers can explain to students that they will listen to the audio recording at the same time that they read along in the text. In some instances, students may then try to read the text, or parts of the text, without the aid of the recording.

The auditory reinforcement of a recording, when combined with the visual image of print, is extremely successful in breaking down barriers for intimidated beginning readers, ESL readers, and readers who are experiencing difficulties. While the focus of this activity is on reading for pleasure, repeated listening and rereading of favorite stories aids fluency, develops sight word vocabulary, and improves story comprehension. For instance, to demonstrate growth in oral reading skills, a teacher can make an audio recording of a student's oral reading at the beginning, middle, and end of the year. The teacher can use the recordings to determine progress, and share them with the student and/or parent if desired.

An audio recorder is a powerful, nonthreatening tool for struggling middle-grade or older students. By having a volunteer record book chapters, students can follow the text at their own pace to work on phrasing, fluency, and comprehension. Some teachers find time to record a single page of text for a poor reader to build fluency and self-esteem – rereading a page she or he already comprehends helps the individual become a better reader. Students can also listen to an assigned recording of a short section of the book, following along in their copy. The next day, they read the section orally to others in a small group. Hearing themselves read fluently is a tremendous confidence booster for all students.

Three Ways to Use Tapes

1. Transcribing
Students can make an audio recording of a conversation between students or during a literature-circle experience, listen to the recording, and transcribe the conversation. The activity highlights for children differences in our spoken and written language.

2. Take-Home Recordings
A system to enable students to borrow audio recordings may be put into place. As an example, children could sign out a tape, DVD, or CD for a period of one week. When they return it, they enter the date returned.

3. Making Audio Books

Fluent readers can make audio recordings of books they have read and would like to share with their classmates. Given that they will need a quiet time for this activity, they can make their recordings at home, using a tape or CD supplied by the school and, if necessary, the means to record. These recordings can also be used in a tutoring or buddy program.

31. Buddy Reading

Buddy or peer reading is a form of shared reading in which one partner reads aloud and another follows along. One partner reads while the other asks questions and retells, or both partners read together. Buddy reading situations may include a teacher and a student, two students with similar reading abilities, or two students with different reading abilities. This section looks at the last form – two students with different abilities.

This form of partnering often comprises a primary student and an older, junior-level reading buddy. Once a week, the two get together. The younger child reads to his or her buddy; the buddy helps out where necessary. Following each session, the pair may complete journal writing and reading activities.

Buddy reading can develop language and literacy in both younger and older students, enhance interpersonal and interaction skills, and improve self-esteem. These programs also benefit teachers, helping them become more reflective as they examine teaching and learning processes shared by pairs of students. Implementing buddy reading programs also allows teachers to witness and observe students in new, involving contexts.

Preparing for a Buddy Reading Program

Teachers can begin by observing students in their class to decide who among them might benefit by participating in a buddy reading program. For each candidate, teachers draw up a short profile that outlines the student's literacy level and interpersonal skills. At the end of September, the teacher meets with the team teacher to pair up buddies.

Older buddies can prepare for their upcoming role by becoming reacquainted with children's literature. The teacher can ask them to read and evaluate several children's books with an aim to establishing a list of recommendations for paired reading sessions. The buddies can work together as a group to discuss quality children's books, and can compare favorite books and authors. Remaining in their group, the teacher can hold mini-lessons on topics relevant to buddy programs; for example, reading aloud, questioning strategies, and stages of child development.

Benefits for Older Buddies

- more skilled, versatile readers
- enhanced social and interpersonal skills
- use of English in natural settings (especially beneficial for ESL students)
- reflection on teaching and skills

Benefits for Younger Buddies

- learn to use a range of reading strategies
- more confident writers and conversationalists
- practise in reading to others
- more skilled at book selection

Pairing Children: What to Consider

Team teachers can discuss each student who is slated to become a part of the buddy reading program and review his or her profile. Younger children who are easily excited or active may require a more patient, mature buddy than a child who is quiet. Teachers can keep in mind that beginning students of English work well with a native speaker of their first language, so these students should be matched whenever possible.

Steps to Implement a Buddy Reading Program

1. Draw up a thorough plan for the initial meeting of the two sets of children. Determine where and when the buddies will meet, and detail activities that will help them get to know each other. (Buddies will need a quiet, private area where they may interact and read.)
2. Set aside a weekly time, which should remain consistent through the year.

3. Younger buddies read to their older buddies, who help out where needed. The two take time to discuss what they are reading or have read.
4. Teachers circulate and make anecdotal notes of their students.
5. Younger buddies, with the help of their older buddies, may write or draw in their reading journals. The two can discuss what has been read, and their ideas, feelings, and thoughts that have been recorded in the journals.
6. Students return to their own classroom to discuss their buddy experience that week. They can write or draw about their time together – accomplishments, positive aspects, problems encountered, and so on. This allows students to celebrate their achievements, share with their peers, and learn from one another. Older students often notice changes in their younger buddy and take pleasure and pride in their development.

32. Choral Reading

Choral reading is group recitation of poetry or prose that allows students to explore together the depth and various meanings of literature in nonthreatening ways. Choral reading allows students to experiment with words and phrases to achieve new and deeper meanings.

It is a useful tool for the classroom, allowing students to explore language without fear, especially shy, withdrawn children or children with speech problems. As a group, students work together to develop appreciation and make meaning of the literature. Choral reading allows opportunities for students to interpret and respond in pleasurable and safe ways.

Students can derive many benefits:

- development of memory skills
- sense of security and unity
- group solidarity
- social skills
- encouragement of trust in groups
- modeling of intonation, rhythm, and beat
- development of visual and auditory memory
- improved reading fluency

Getting Started

Younger students need to be taught choral reading using a simple rote process. Short, lively poems work well.

1. The teacher reads the selection to the students.
2. She or he rereads the poem and discusses its words with students. Is the poem funny? spooky?
3. The teacher reads it again and asks students to join in on specific parts or words of the poem.
4. The students join in as much as they can every time the teacher reads the poem.
5. The teacher lessens the amount she or he reads aloud until the students are reading alone.

Even young children can handle relatively sophisticated material. The success of the activity depends on the interests and skills of the teacher.

As students begin to read, the teacher can start working from a script, which can be written on the board, an overhead, or chart paper. She or he can encourage students to mark up the script. Choral reading is easily integrated into the daily routine of class activities; for example, students can read from overheads, charts, chalkboards, big books, and songs. The teacher may want to prepare a daily message that the students choral read.

Methods of Arranging Poems for Choral Reading

1. *Two-Part Arrangement:* One group of voices balances with another, with each group speaking alternately.
2. *Soloist and Chorus:* One student reads a specific stanza or lines – the rest join in on other lines.
3. *Line a Child:* One pair of students reads a line or couplet, the next pair reads the next lines, and so on. The reading ends with all students speaking the last line or couplet.
4. *Increasing/Decreasing Volume:* Take away or add voices as readers build up or move away from the climax of the poem.
5. *Increasing/Decreasing Tempo:* Increase or decrease the speed as the poem is recited.
6. *Unison:* The whole group speaks as one.
7. *Effects:* Accompany the choral reading with music, movement, and sound effects.
8. *Divide into Groups:* Each group comes up with its own interpretation of the poem.

Methods of Presenting Poems for Choral Reading

For Younger Students
1. Write the text on chart paper.
2. Divide the poem into parts.
3. Discuss different ways the poem may be read. Discuss the author's intent, and the mood, language, rhythm, meter, rhyme, and use of alliteration.
4. Provide time for students to rehearse.
5. Place students in groups. They may be positioned so that different voices come from different places within the group.
6. Rehearse the reading of the poem as a whole.
7. Perform the choral reading for other classes, parents, community groups, etc.

For Older Students
1. Introduce the poem; talk about the subject; then read it to class.
2. Reread the poem. Discuss important points.
3. Begin by reciting the first few lines.
4. Encourage students to mark up the scripts by underlining key words, pauses, etc.
5. Read the first two lines together, then the next two, then the four together.
6. Increase this amount until the whole poem is finished.
7. Over the next few days, continue to recite the poem until the students have mastered it. Introduce movement, costume, and art.

Ways to Read A Poem Aloud

1. Echo Reading
The teacher says one part; the students repeat what the teacher says.

Teacher: *I never saw a purple cow,*
Students: *I never saw a purple cow,*
Teacher: *I hope I never see one;*
Students: *I hope I never see one,*
Teacher: *But I can tell you, anyhow,*
Students: *But I can tell you, anyhow,*
Teacher: *I'd rather see than be one.*
Students: *I'd rather see than be one.*

2. Alternate Reading
The teacher says one line; the students say the next line.

Teacher: *I never saw a purple cow,*
Students: *I hope I never see one:*

Teacher: *But I can tell you, anyhow,*
Students: *I'd rather see than be one.*

3. Unison
Once the students are familiar with the rhyme, they can say the poem aloud together at the same time. The teacher can join in as a member of the group.

All: *I never saw a purple cow,*
I hope I never see one:
But I can tell you, anyhow,
I'd rather see than be one.

4. Two Groups
The class is divided into two groups (each half of the room; boy voices/ girl voices; by birthdays for the first half of the year/ the latter part of the year); the groups read alternate lines. Repeating a reading of a selection with each group reversing parts works well.

Group One: *I never saw a purple cow,*
Group Two: *I hope I never see one;*
Group One: *But I can tell you, anyhow,*
Group Two: *I'd rather see than be one.*
Or by dividing each of the lines:
Group One: *I never saw*
Group Two: *a purple cow*
Group One: *I hope*
Group Two: *I never see one.*

5. Assignment of lines
The class can be divided into groups, with each group assigned a line of the selection or a verse of a longer selection. Also, individual students can be assigned a line, a part of a line, or a word to contribute to the shared reading of the poem.

Group One: *I never saw a purple cow*
Group Two: *I hope I never see one:*
Group Three: *But I can tell you, anyhow,*
Group Four: *I'd rather see than be one.*

Or

Student #1: *I*
Student #2: *never*
Student #3: *saw*
Student #4: *a*

6. Different voices

The words of the selection can be said in a whisper or in loud voices. Or, the lines can be said gradually going from soft to loud or from loud to soft. Similarly, students can say the poem slowly to quickly.

7. Rhythm clapping

As students say the lines, they clap along with the rhythm of the selection (or tap knees, or snap fingers). They can also clap hands with a partner as they say the poem aloud.

8. Singing

Some rhymes can be song to familiar tunes. For instance "The Purple Cow" could be sung to the tune of "Row, Row, Row Your Boat."

33. Drama and Literacy

Learning Through Drama

Drama is a shared learning experience and collaborative group effort – the threads of individual response are woven together to build an improvised world in which all students share. Drama reveals and provides skills for negotiating problems of classroom dynamics and interpersonal relationships. It can enhance individual and group self-esteem – children with learning exceptionalities often experience great success with drama. As we make sense of others' stories, we come closer to understanding our own.

Situations, characters, problems, relationships, mood, atmosphere, texture, and concepts of a story can be explored extensively. Teachers think deeply about the story, trying to understand and consider its broadest themes and ideas. Questions they ask students must prod them toward these elements, and move from the particular experience of the story to a more general understanding of the nature of what is being explored.

When a teacher puts himself or herself in role, children understand that the focus is not on the individual's response or contribution, but on the problem before the class and the process of resolving it. This is a powerful technique teachers have at their disposal to guide the drama.

Structures allow students to find new insights and understanding. They will feel most committed if they understand and accept the plan for the drama, and ideally they should eventually contribute to the planning. Teachers must listen, watch, and set up situations that provide lots of room for exploration in a specific direction.

Setting the Stage

Games, particularly cooperative games, can help promote a positive classroom climate and strong community among children. Teachers need to recognize the importance of negotiation and can make their classroom a place where students expect to be listened to, where their contributions are valued by the teacher and by their peers.

Teachers new to drama can begin by using simple dialogue, and questions and answers, in role. They can ask students to respond as if they are a character from a story being read aloud. Gradually, they can move into "what if," speculations based on what they've imagined – tried and true stories are sure to elicit imaginative response. Keeping students in a circle is a good management technique that provides perimeters for the activity and allows all to be equal participants. The teacher may want to devise a signal to indicate when the work will begin and end. Students can work in pairs, in small groups, or as a large group; the more students actively involved at any one time, the better. When possible, role playing can begin with a whole-group activity, move into small and individual work situations, and end with a whole-group situation.

A drama can last for one session or extend in a unit through many, depending on the interest of the students and the possibilities inherent in the themes or materials with which the group or class is working. A teacher may extend a unit through a number of interlocking dramatizations that take place in different times and places, or under different conditions, researching or reflecting in various ways between these events. Students' thinking will deepen over time.

A teacher will collectively decide when the drama is over, based on his or her satisfaction with the outcome of events. Often, a teacher will try to keep the students from rushing to a resolution of the problem in the drama by challenging superficial responses, pressing for elaboration, and extending thoughtless or sloppy contributions. Belief and commitment in drama on the teacher's part passes on to students the importance and power of words and language.

1. Familiar Stories

One of the easiest ways to begin story dramatization is to have students in small groups dramatize familiar stories using their own words and movements. They include all major aspects of the plot, but supply their own details and dialogue. Space must always be made for extrapolation and interpretation to allow for learning. (A limitation of retellings, in their true form, is that they ask children to focus on details and sequence – in effect, the surface of the story.) When students have dramatized the story, they can explore events that might have occurred before or after it, or change its locale, time, and mood.

2. Tableaux

Tableaux or sculptures can be used to develop the context of drama. Have students act out an activity. On a prearranged signal, they freeze. Creating tableaux or asking students to move in slow motion is also a good way to control the action in more extended dramas – you can slow them for a detailed discussion, or get them moving if a discussion has gone on too long. You can introduce tableaux work by having students work together in small groups to form a single shape, such as a geometric shape or a symbol (e.g., a letter, a number, the answer to an addition or subtraction problem). Tableaux work can be extended by allowing each student to speak one word, later speaking phrases or sentences that best express their, or their characters', feelings.

3. Extended Role Playing

If you feel you and the class might be ready for more extended role play, it may be useful to carefully explain what you will be attempting before you start. "Going into role" can become a familiar phrase. You might want to set the situation and scene clearly. At first, students might be more comfortable staying themselves and questioning you in role. You might want to give them some time to think about the characters they will become. Tell them to close their eyes and silently decide the answers to questions: How old

are you? Where do you live? What are you wearing? Are you kind/angry/miserable/frightened?

4. Interviews

Interviews provide an opportunity to plan questions related to a text's author and/or illustrator, or a character from a text. Prior to planning and role playing interviews, you can introduce students to the topic of interview structure and the types of questioning techniques that elicit desired responses.

- *Character interviews:* These interviews allow students to respond creatively to narrative, factual, and poetic text. They can explore character and make meaning by role playing a character from a text. This activity is most effective when students work in pairs, with each taking turns to play a character and his or her interviewer. When finished, each pair decides on the most effective role play and presents it to the rest of the class.

- *Character panel interviews:* Following the reading of a text, students decide to be reporters or characters from the story. Each interviewer prepares a series of questions related to one of the characters; each character prepares a series of responses in relation to possible questions from the interviewer. After the role playing, students can compare their lists of questions to determine similarities and differences.

- *Interview the author or illustrator:* Select a text or a range of texts, and ask students to find a partner. In pairs, they plan a series of questions they would like to ask the text's author and/or illustrator. As a class, students can pool their questions, draw up a list of the five most commonly asked questions, and submit them to the author or illustrator, care of the publisher.

After the Drama

After the drama, students have the chance to explain and analyze the actions and decisions they made. This form of thought, discussion, and writing makes conscious the learning that occurred during the drama.

After drama work, it is useful to have a large-group discussion about involvement, in which the teacher can explain that an individual's commitment and level of activity within the drama can vary for different reasons, and that everyone must consider how their behavior has, or had, the potential to affect the result.

Strategies for Reading Scripts

Scripts are useful resources for moving students into oral reading. They can be found in some reading anthologies, as excerpts from published films and TV programs, and as models written by older students.

1. Students are assigned roles to read aloud. Once they are familiar with their lines, they can exchange characters and read the new character's lines.
2. The students read the script aloud as a group, each person reading one sentence at time. Stage directions can be ignored for this read-aloud activity.
3. Each student selects one word or phrase from each speech his or her character says. The scene can be rehearsed with each student saying only that word or phrase.
4. Students can experiment with different styles to add fresh insights to the scene; for example, rehearse the scene as if it were a western movie, a science fiction movie, a television cartoon, a soap opera.
5. At any time during rehearsal, before memorization, the students can put the scripts aside and improvise the scene. Students can then discuss what changes they made to the script; they can decide which lines have been internalized and which have been neglected.
6. Students can listen to an audio recording of the scene, and consider what revisions might be needed to make their interpretation most effective.

---

34. Readers Theatre

Readers theatre, related to both oral reading and story drama, occurs when two or more people read the dialogue of a story in role. Often a narrator reads the narration, or the group chooses to read it together as a chorus. There are many creative ways in which narration can be done, as long as the script is read with expression, since little or no body movement is used in readers theatre. Instead, emphasis is placed on vocal performance.

The use of props, if any, is kept to a minimum. However, because young children are less inhibited, the use of simple props, such as a hat, book, or purse, may be encouraged. Their use will make the presentation enjoyable for both readers and their audience. When appropriate, the audience can be invited to participate in the performance in some way, perhaps by providing necessary sound effects.

Although readers theatre requires less practice than a play, students still require rehearsal time. Teachers may want to read the script aloud to the children and then have them read through it and practise it several times before the presentation. Once students are familiar and comfortable with the use of prepared scripts, they can write their own!

Benefits of Working with Readers Theatre

- Language is an active and meaning-based activity. As young people read, cast, rehearse, and perform a script they are involved in a engaging, active process.
- Readers theatre is inclusive. It can successfully involve all readers at different stages of development. It allows struggling readers, reluctant readers, and ESL learners to focus on short pieces of text, and promotes success as students are supported by others to read their parts aloud.
- Repeated readings of scripts offers young readers an incentive to improve their reading for an audience. Rehearsal is the essence of readers theatre, helping students get practice in becoming fluent oral readers.
- When working with readers theatre, students learn to hear themselves. They try to improve their reading to emulate the best reading models they have heard from their parents, from their teachers, or on audio recordings.
- As students rehearse and prepare a performance, they explore literature in a new form; they can examine character, plot development, and story grammar of the text. It is an interpretive dramatic process where students go inside a story to experience the thoughts and feelings of the characters.

- Listening skills are strengthened as students continue to practise, revise, listen to the opinions of others, and critique their own work. The process also promotes active listening for those who are in the audience.
- Readers theatre is an authentic cooperative activity. Each member needs to recognize that all readers are needed to produce a polished successful performance.
- Discipline and commitment is required of each participant during the preparation of a readers theatre performance, as well as during the performance itself.
- Because no overt sets, props, or costumes are used, the only way for students to convey meaning is through their voices. Reading with meaning and expression improves a student's fluency.
- Readers theatre is an accessible strategy for presenting drama work within a program or performance. The process of rehearsing can be a pleasurable activity for students; it can be a rewarding celebration for participants as they successfully perform for other classes or families.
- Readers theatre gives students success in reading and sharing. Such success is highly motivating for the reader, who learns to appreciate the different forms of reading.

35. Reading Journals

A reading journal is a notebook in which students record their personal reactions to, questions about, and reflections on what they have read, viewed, listened to, and discussed. As well, they reflect on the strategies they use when taking part in these activities.

Reading journals serve a number of purposes:

- they help connect reading and writing, enabling children to see literacy as a whole
- they promote critical thinking and affective response
- they help develop interpretive skills and organize simple recountings
- they offer a record of their reactions to a literature selection or to a group discussion, to be reflected on at a later time

- they encourage a range of responses beyond literal questions and answers
- they facilitate thoughtful and personal responses to what has been read
- they offer a means of reacting during the reading of a selection, and not just at its completion
- they support follow-up discussion activities
- they present opportunities for examining words and language patterns used by authors – slang, idioms, unusual or unknown words
- they invite open-ended questions that promote further discussion
- they offer opportunities for assessment, weekly and throughout the year, as children reread and reflect on their entries
- they establish opportunities for independent work while the teacher assists other groups

See BLM on page 118.

Using Reading Journals

Teachers can set aside twenty minutes of reading time and ten minutes for journal writing. They can display a list of possible starters that students have formulated previously; for example:

I was surprised when _____ .
I predict that _____ will happen next because _____.
The story reminds me of the time I _____ .

Typically, students who are unfamiliar with the format and purpose of response journals summarize the plot of the story they have read. As they become more familiar with the concept, their entries gain in insight, particularly those written in response to whole-class readings.

Dialogue Journals

In dialogue journals, the teacher and students participate in weekly open, written conversations about a book the children are reading, in order to share interpretations and viewpoints. The teacher must be sensitive to the beginning efforts of the students, and think of the entries as conversations around books. Because the teacher is part of the dialogue, students are often highly motivated to participate. She or he responds to what the students have written, elaborating or extending their entries, answering their questions, and asking questions the students might consider. In some instances, the teacher may have to establish a minimum or maximum number of sentences to develop the rhythm of dialogue journals. Both teacher and student are free to choose what to write about and whether or not to respond, and are considered equal in the exchange. Dialogue journals provide a good opportunity for teachers to model writing skills. By working with three or four students a day, the teacher can quickly dialogue with the whole class within a few days.

Tips for Teachers

- Support the student's message. Connect with what the students have said in some way, whether by acknowledging, agreeing, or sharing similar ideas.
- Provide information. This is important when an entry indicates that a student misunderstands or lacks facts.
- Clarify and extend thinking. When an entry is unclear, ask for clarification. Challenge students to rethink, reflect, and stretch their minds.
- Provide questions to answer as prompts.
- Write about your reading and share your responses with students. Let them know that you have favorite writers and genres.
- Respond in writing to students. Since journals are not assignments, they should not be given a mark or grade. They must feel free to write their true responses to their readings.
- Ask students to share entries with one another and with you. The response journal is a good source for discussion in student–teacher conferences and in peer reading groups.
- Ask students to keep track of what they have read and to evaluate the books and their entries. They can also fill in graphs to show how much time they spend reading.

Questions to Choose from to Motivate Reading Responses

1. When you first chose your book (before you had read it), what kind of book did you think it would be?
2. Now that you have finished it, how did it fit your expectations?
3. What did you like best about the book?
4. What will you tell your friends about the book?
5. What puzzles grew from reading this book?
6. Have you read any other books like this one?
7. What surprises happened during the book?
8. Did you read this book a chapter at a time? Did you read it all the way through? Did you leave it for a while?
9. Do you think you will read it again?
10. If there were a film made about this book, would you want to see it?
11. Whose voice speaks to you most strongly in this book? Was that person the book's main character?
12. Who was telling the story?
13. When did the story take place? Did it matter where it took place?
14. How long did it take for the whole story to happen?
15. Were there any flashbacks, flashforwards, or time warps?
16. What places were described in the story?
17. Would you like to have been inside this story as it was happening?
18. When did you feel as if you were actually inside the story?
19. When did you feel you were staring at the characters as an observer?
20. Did you hope that an event would not happen, but it happened anyway?
21. Did anything ever happen to you just as it happened in this story?
22. If a time warp occurred and you found yourself in the book, which character would you choose to become?
23. When you are reading, do you see pictures in your mind?
24. What would you like to do now to help you think about your book?
25. Which friend would you give this book to for a birthday present?
26. Do you like to sketch as you read – drawing the pictures that play in your mind?
27. How would you have handled the problems characters faced in your book?
28. What do you think the author was trying to tell you about life in this book?
29. Do you agree with the way the author thinks about life as described in this book?
30. What would you ask the author of this book?
31. When were you "hooked" by this book and realized you would read it all the way through?

32. Go back and look at the cover. How accurate is it now that you know the story?
33. Reread the blurb on the back cover. Is it fair?
34. What kind of music could you play for a friend to get him or her into the right mood to read this book?
35. What did you learn from reading this book that you hadn't thought about before?
36. What was special about the way the author used language in this book?
37. Was there anything unusual about the style of the book?
38. What quotations would you choose from this book to put on the wall of your classroom?
39. What special words do you remember?
40. When did you have your strongest feeling while reading this book?

36. Cloze Procedures

In 1953, Wilson Taylor derived the word "cloze" from the Gestalt psychology term, "closure."

Cloze procedure involves oral or written deletions of parts of words, whole words, or phrases in a passage of text. "Clozing," or restoring these gaps, requires students to scan the text, recognize and process contextual cues, and then choose the most appropriate word. The reader learns to use context to help figure out unfamiliar words. It's an active, constructive language process.

A Cloze Passage

The cabin was buried deep (in) the woods. The water came from a (well) dug into the earth. Old trees were cut into (logs), and bushes were full (of) juicy berries. The birds sang each (morning) and the brown squirrels (gathered) acorns.

Cloze activities are suitable for use at all grade levels and help to build a number of skills exhibited by strong, fluent readers. They focus on contextual cueing systems, strengthening the readers' abilities to anticipate the text to make the most sense.

Children interact with text – searching, scanning, and thinking – which may result in making meaning with print. Cloze can help expand the readers' repertoires of thinking strategies.

Cloze activities can increase the readers' confidence – as they experience success with cloze, readers realize that they can predict in order to recognize words – and are useful for assessing students' reading ability, comprehension, and vocabulary awareness.

Designing a Cloze Activity

1. Deletions can target particular words or can be made arbitrarily by formula (e.g., every fifth word). Teachers can also tailor cloze exercises by
   - deleting parts of words, whole words, or phrases;
   - retaining words that are structurally interdependent;
   - providing visual aids (e.g., the first letter of each deleted word) when introducing the written cloze to young students;
   - using dashes, boxes, or numbers in brackets to indicate the number of letters deleted.
2. Along with the teacher's choice of text and students' knowledge and literacy levels, the selected deletions will strongly influence the difficulty of a cloze activity. Teachers need to consider that
   - content words, such as nouns and verbs, are more difficult to predict than structure words, such as articles.
   - deletions at the beginning of a sentence are more difficult to predict than those made at its middle or end.
   - difficulty increases with the number of deletions made.
3. To maximize the learning benefits of cloze activities, teachers can structure a lesson to focus on the *process* of restoring deletions, as opposed to the end product. In pairs, small groups, or as a class, students generate, discuss, debate, justify, compare, and select possible solutions for each deletion. The author's original choice is only useful when presented as a focus for discussion: Why might the author have chosen this word or phrase?
4. Independent activities (e.g., worksheets) may not capitalize on the potential for learning. Teachers can combine independent cloze work

with group discussion, and pair or group students with varying abilities.

5. Written cloze can be presented in a variety of ways. An enlarged reproduction can be prepared for a whole-class activity. Pairs or groups can use worksheets before gathering as a class to share, compare, and discuss selections. (When designing worksheets, teachers need to leave room for multiple suggestions at each deletion.)

6. For oral cloze, teachers read aloud and pause at deletions so students can brainstorm, record, and discuss predictions. Illustrations can be used as visual cues. (Many of us present oral cloze regularly – predicting what will happen next in a story is cloze!)

7. Students can ask themselves these questions when attempting to select words:
   - What is this text about?
   - What kind of text is this?
   - What is the author trying to say?
   - How is the author trying to say it?
   - Why does this make sense?
   - Is that the way we would say it?
   - Why would that word work?
   - What other words could we use?

37. Using Graphic Organizers

See BLMs on pages 119–126.

Mind Maps

Mind maps are visual tools that enable learners to make connections among ideas and concepts, assisting the learner in seeing relationships and patterns in their thinking. The structure of mind maps is similar to the way the brain sorts and stores information. These graphic organizers can facilitate the development of metacognition, helping students to be conscious of their own thinking strategies during the act of problem solving. Not only can mind maps deepen students' understanding of the concepts they are learning, but they also can provide opportunities for educators to gain valuable insight into their students' learning. Mind maps can help the brain to organize ideas and think more creatively.

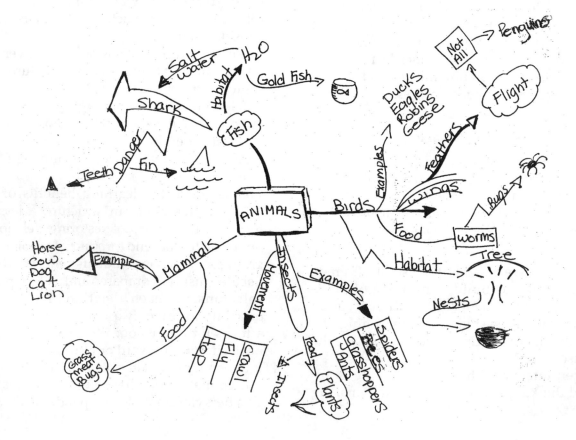

Components of a Mind Map

1. Images
A mind map always has a central image that represents the main topic of the map. The images help the brain to think more creatively and store ideas more readily in long-term memory. Images can also be included in other areas in the mind map (on the lines, beside words, etc.) to represent ideas and key themes.

2. Lines
In a mind map, lines radiate like branches from the central image. They are used to create connections between related concepts; they can be any style or thickness.

3. Words
One or two words are usually written on the connector lines in order to identify key concepts or ideas. The words can be any size or style.

4. Color
As mind maps usually include a variety of subtopics branching out from a central topic, color can help to organize the map and make it easier to read. Similar ideas or themes can be connected using the same color for lines and/or words.

When creating mind maps, invite students to begin by representing the main topic (usually by an image and/or word) in the middle of their page. From the central topic, related ideas radiate out in the form of lines, words, and images. Mind maps are hierarchical in nature, so the concepts and ideas should become more specific the further they are placed from the central image.

Encourage your students to integrate different line styles in their maps. Images can be placed anywhere in the map to highlight specific concepts or words. Encourage your students to use color to organize similar ideas and themes.

Ten Mind-Map Activities

1. Students can create a mind map while they listen to a story. Encourage students to include the details and images they feel are important. Students can then share and compare their maps with others.

2. Before reading a novel or picture book, invite students to create a mind map on what they think the story will be about. Then, once they have read the story, invite them to revisit their map and explore the similarities and differences in their predictions.

3. After reading or listening to a poem, the students to can create a mind map on what the poem means to them.

4. Invite students to create a cooperative mind map about the characters in a book they have read. Each person in the group can complete a section of the mind map for a different character.

5. Organize your class into small groups. Each group begins a mind map on a different book the class has read (or on a different topic they have studied). Once they have added some details to their map, invite the students to move to another map and add their ideas to it. Students keep changing maps until each group has had an opportunity to add their ideas to each map. Once each group returns to their original map, they can view the new ideas that have been added and continue to add their own.

6. Invite students to create a story using a mind map. They can include the characters , as well as the events that will take place. Invite students to tell the story using the mind map.

7. Invite students to create a mind map about a book they have read. Then, in pairs, students can share their mind maps with each other, comparing and contrasting the characters and/or themes in their books.

8. Create a mind map with your students. The map can be about a book they have read, or a topic they have studied or are about to study. Invite students to decide on the topics, themes, etc. to include in the map. Engage students in adding lines, words, and images where they feel appropriate.

9. As part of a research project, invite students to share what they have learned in the form of a mind map.

10. Invite students to map out what they know and do not know about a specific topic. Students can share their maps with each other. Once they have completed a unit of study on the topic, students can review their maps and make changes based on what they have learned.

It is important to keep in mind that mind mapping is a creative process that enables students to represent their thinking and make new connections in their learning. No two mind maps are identical, as they are personal representations of how an individual organizes and expresses their understanding of a specific topic.

Venn Diagrams

A Venn diagram is an effective and concise graphic tool employed in post-reading contexts. It can represent comparisons and contrasting information within one story or book (e.g., settings) or between two or more books. A Venn diagram consists of two or more overlapping circles: the parts of the circles that do not intersect represent unique or contrasting attributes, while the intersected sections depict shared or common characteristics that can be compared.

Plot Organizers

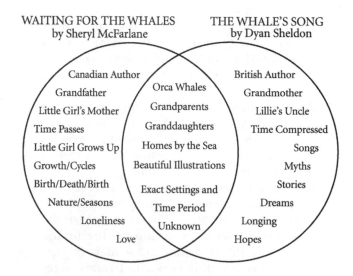

WAITING FOR THE WHALES
by Sheryl McFarlane

THE WHALE'S SONG
by Dyan Sheldon

Canadian Author
Grandfather
Little Girl's Mother
Time Passes
Little Girl Grows Up
Growth/Cycles
Birth/Death/Birth
Nature/Seasons
Loneliness
Love

Orca Whales
Grandparents
Granddaughters
Homes by the Sea
Beautiful Illustrations
Exact Settings and
Time Period
Unknown

British Author
Grandmother
Lillie's Uncle
Time Compressed
Songs
Myths
Stories
Dreams
Longing
Hopes

Plot organizers, an example of a post-reading activity, provide a visual means for organizing and analyzing plots, and can often be geared directly to specific types of texts. These organizers help children summarize a plot and understand its organization, and they act as models for children writing their own stories.

While there are at least four types of graphic plot organizers, pictures tend to take too much space and tend to be challenging to depict in words. Instead it is easier for the reader to refer directly to the text.

Notwithstanding the lack of visual aids, specific plot organizers (e.g., circular, stair-step) directly complement, represent, and heighten particular recurring plot patterns (e.g., circular, cumulative, count down) found in children's books. Plot-profile line graphs and cut-and-paste grids are examples of organizers in which children rate events on books using horizontal and vertical axes (events – horizontal; rating – vertical). Students' illustrations often accompany these organizers.

38. Working with Art

Having students respond to readings with artwork is useful for checking comprehension and interest among ESL, kindergarten, and early primary students, children who are shy, or children with poorly developed language skills. However, drawing is not just for those who can't write fluently, and creating pictures is not just rehearsal for real writing. For readers of any age, images are part of the serious business of making meaning – partners with words for communicating our inner designs.

Students of all ages can draw along with their writing and their responses to stories. Linking visual with verbal modes of expression will result in better description and detail. There are many ways to see – teachers can capitalize on students' multiple intelligences. Making pictures gives children a sense of freedom of expression because they feel less restricted by rules and convention than when they write without pictures. Making pictures, along with writing, leads to poetic, complex, expressive, imaginative, reflective writing.

1. An Artists' Workshop
Use the workshop approach by asking students to write journals about their artwork, not only to show meaning in their pictures, but to express their thinking, observations, ideas on assessments and revisions, description of process, future plans, and reflections on their learning.

2. Art Stimulates More Writing
Cut and laminate quality art work from calendars, magazines, catalogues, and journals. Cover the

classroom with these prints before students arrive. When they enter the class, ask them to pretend they are in an art gallery. The purpose of their visit is to choose four pictures that they will incorporate into a story. Suggest that they select one or two character pictures, one setting picture, and one event picture. To all their questions, answer, "You decide." Have them write narratives including characters, setting, problem, and solution to problem. Their narratives will be rich and complex, with tension created by unusual pictures that lift their stories.

3. Explore Picture Books
What relationship exists between the visual and verbal in picture books? Could one stand without the other? Do they tell the same story? Do they interpret the story creatively? Have the students provide alternative illustrations for a favorite story book, or write an alternative text for favorite illustrations in a picture book. They can also create picture books for younger readers.

4. Ways to Respond and Retell
Students can respond to and retell stories using masks, silhouettes, puppets, collages, quilts, student-made costumes, weavings, dolls, mobiles, posters, and dioramas. They can create a photo essay or home video version of the story, perhaps asking fellow students to act out key scenes. As teachers, we need to strive to provide a variety of artistic media and encourage a variety of artistic techniques.

5. Making Books
Display for children a range of books – big, small, miniature, shape, pop-up, fold-out, see-through, flip, cloth, rebus, and code books. Students can use one or more as a model to create their own book, using a story they have written as its base.

6. Place Slogan Here
Students can promote their favorite book by designing stamps, stickers, bookmarks, calendars, badges, place mats, sandwich boards, postcards, plaques, and playing cards that tell others of its merits.

7. Sketch to Stretch
Have students use drawing as an intermediary step between reading a text and discussion. They can share their sketches in small groups , as other members speculate on the artist's intent before listening to his or her interpretation. Finally one student can elect to share his or her sketch with the entire class in the same manner. When finished, discuss with them reasons for varying interpretations of text. Emphasize that these differences are to be expected.

39. Parallel Reading

After a story experience, students will often meet more stories that illuminate, clarify, or open up the original narrative. We may begin with just one particular story with a class but, before long, the students have found a dozen more, some hidden in the recesses of their story minds, some discovered in the library, some invented through storytelling sessions, and others created collaboratively through story-building activities. As teachers, we also add our own selections, some to be read or told aloud, others to be left on a table to be read by volunteers. One story gives birth to a thousand. We read what the original texts suggest and connect to.

Parallel reading can occur in a variety of situations:

- reading author stories by the same author or illustrator
- reading other stories connected to the theme, concept, style, or culture of the original
- locating background information and research by reading about the author or illustrator
- reading non-fiction stories that relate to the story
- finding reviews and reports about the book, the time, the setting, or the author
- reading related stories written by other children

Story Sets

It can be an exciting adventure for students to meet literary versions of a story they think they know. Suddenly, their preconceptions are jolted, and they move into an altered state, caught in a web of changing perception, noticing every minute difference. The "story brain" is engaged.

When children experience two or more stories that are related in some way, their understanding of each is altered and enriched by the other, as they make connections between their expanding lives and the stories. Often one story prepares the reader for another one, facilitating the understanding of the subsequent story. And, of course, each new story sheds light on past story experiences, creating a changing view of the stories in the child's story repertoire.

Children can meet all kinds of different stories and then focus on similarities and differences; individuals can each read a different story, and then share their understandings and findings. There are many ways to organize the sharing of different but related stories:

- comparison charts, which demonstrate particular characteristics within different categories
- samples of specific language peculiarities
- emotional responses
- analyses of artistic interpretations
- variations in story structures, settings, cultures, or resolutions

As we journey along story pathways, we may suddenly find a story we passed appearing with new life and new vitality.

Part E: The Reading Workshop

40. Language-Rich Resources

- Novels – contemporary and classic – at different reading levels, added to throughout the year
- Non-fiction by authors who craft their writing
- Publishers' anthologies – full of useful, short selections for working in small groups
- Picture books that offer students in the middle years an aesthetic experience with words and visuals
- Magazines, both to be read and to be used as art resources for responding and creating
- Audio recorded versions of books of all kinds, for struggling readers and for gifted readers
- Interactive computer software and the Internet
- Poetry anthologies to be read and listened to, which would be undiscovered unless we introduce them
- Letters, memos, and advertisements to use in our demonstrations
- Student writing that highlights the writer's craft or that represents emotional power
- Teacher writing that illustrates who we are as learners
- Bits and pieces saved from the texts of our lives that we need to share with our students
- Songs to be read aloud as we sing the lyrics together
- Book talks, discussions, guest speakers, video clips – voices from outside the walls that resonate within
- Jokes, riddles, puns, funny anecdotes, riddles, tongue twisters, rhymes – all representing the play of language
- Selections from newspapers students may not find in their homes, along with articles and reviews from free community newspapers and magazines
- References, such as dictionaries, thesauruses, writing handbooks, books of quotations, etc.
- Computer programs, software, and Internet connections

41. Reading Aloud to Students

Reading to children encourages literacy, promotes reading skills, and contributes to the sharing of the joy of literature. As children listen and respond to literature, they predict, make inferences, hypothesize, identify with the characters, respond critically and creatively, and develop a sense of story. Stories read aloud can be above the class's reading level, exposing them to an even greater range of literacy.

A one-on-one school reading activity (based on the home bedtime lap-reading experience) usually occurs between a teacher and student, but it can also occur with an older reading buddy or a parent volunteer. As the student listens to the story being read aloud, she or he begins to notice the words on the page. By following the eyes of the reader, the student understands that books are read from top to bottom and left to right. As she or he hears and sees the words of a favorite book, the student notices that some words occur repeatedly, leading eventually to recognition of these words. This recognition also stems from familiarity with known words in specific contexts. A whole-class shared reading experience is a natural extension of the one-on-one lap-reading activity.

Reading aloud can alter a student's attitudes to and appreciation of the developing journey toward literacy. The teacher models the joy of reading and the satisfaction that comes from making meaning with print. A student who cannot read well is able to understand orally the stories and articles that are brought to life by a willing teacher, building vocabulary and sentence patterns through the ear, and connecting what she or he hears to printed text. Students benefit from listening to stories and books read aloud, from repeated readings of favorite books in the primary years to book talks, demonstrations, and the sharing of excerpts and poems in the senior years. Hearing text read aloud allows students to focus on how various types of text work and how authors work in the writing process. Students who have limited reading ability can still appreciate the text and join in a variety of response activities. Examples include forming discussion groups, working at thematic centers, taking part in whole-class drama, working from within the book's story frame, and learning how readers seem to function.

When teachers read aloud to students, they act as language role models. A teacher can read aloud a variety of literature forms, including folk tales, stories, poetry, and biographies. Students should have the chance to experience hundreds of books through their teacher's voice to provide opportunities for language and concept development.

Preparing for Reading Aloud

1. Use books suited to the students' age level. Often, older children have not considered reading picture books, but enjoy experiencing them when teachers read aloud.
2. Choose books that are appropriate and relevant to the needs and wants of the class.
3. Develop performance strategies that invite students into the story:
   - use dynamic shifts in volume,
   - fluctuate the timbre and tone of your voice,
   - develop character voices that can be used in a number of stories,
   - find places to pause and ask questions or make observations,
   - understand the stories you plan to read.
4. Rehearse the stories you plan to read.
5. Develop a repertoire of practised stories for rereading.

Reading aloud can be integrated into a curriculum in many ways. For example, when working on a unit about exploration, a teacher can include books about the Franklin expedition, space pioneers, or mountaineering in the Himalayas. When involved in a novel study, a teacher can read excerpts from books similar in theme to those being read by the students.

Invite Authors

Local authors can be invited to visit the school and share their reading and writing experiences. Students enjoy these visits where they get to meet a "real" author and can ask him or her questions about writing, being a writer, and favorite stories.

Sharing Stories

A variety of guests from the community (e.g., hairdressers, doctors, athletes) can be invited to serve as reading role models by preparing a story to read to the class, supporting the idea that all kinds of people are readers – not just teachers and librarians, but people who read because they want to. Older students, parents, teachers, senior citizens, and other members of the community can share stories.

Students can participate as storytellers by creating and completing their own stories and preparing a tape of themselves reading. The final version of the taped story is then made available at the listening centre for others to enjoy. Pairing individuals can create some interesting, creative results. Further, some children may be inspired to dramatize or videotape their work.

42. Storytelling

By watching the listeners in a storytelling session, a teacher can come to a new understanding, and share with the students an enriching experience. The pleasure that arises between speaker and listener rests on the teller's interpretation, which may stimulate the listener's imagination to set the scene, visualize the players, and follow the action. The voice, expression, gestures, and imagination of the storyteller are powerful factors in determining whether the audience experiences a story vividly and creatively.

Storyteller Bob Barton's Suggestions

1. Read the story slowly. Make an outline of it in your own words and retell it to yourself.
2. Read the story a second time to check that you have not left out any important details.
3. Read the story a third time and consider the feelings and attitudes of its characters. Tell the story to yourself again.
4. On the fourth reading, pay attention to the language of the story. What words or phrases should be preserved to retain the story's unique sound? Tell the story again to yourself.
5. A fifth reading might be devoted to blocking the story into scenes and considering the sensory details (e.g., lights, sounds, color). Now tell the story to yourself again.
6. During your final reading, concentrate on the beginning and ending. A strong start and a confident finish are important: you may want to memorize the beginning and ending of the story.
7. You can employ various editing techniques (e.g., condensing the story; elaborating on a small point; converting dialogue to narrative, or vice versa; rearranging the plot, particularly if the story's exposition is long).

Insight into the kind of shaping a story requires becomes more apparent after you have told yourself the story a few times.

8. The real test of your telling comes when you face your audience. Storytelling is an audience-valuing situation. The storyteller should feel the audience response throughout and modify the delivery accordingly. The important thing is to start slowly, observe the responses of your listeners, and maintain your concentration. See your story, feel it – make everything happen. Use the voice you use in everyday conversation and respond naturally to your feelings about the story. As for gestures and body language, let them be natural as well. With practice you will learn what is right for your style and delivery.

43. Shared Reading

Procedures for teaching with shared reading are based on observations of the way children learn to read during bedtime or lap-story reading experiences in the home. In a shared reading experience at school, reading becomes an enjoyable social activity when an entire class reads collectively. Through cooperative learning, students can tackle texts that are slightly beyond their developmental stage.

The teacher, through the shared reading experience, provides input and a supportive, motivating atmosphere in order to facilitate the construction of knowledge. Students are considered "doers" as readers; the reading experience furthers their lives in the here and now because it is an enjoyable and social activity; and they are free to take risks in a safe, encouraging atmosphere. Young readers, through a shared reading experience, make meaning as story, images, words, sounds, and rhymes combine and complement one another in a collaborative group setting. While shared reading experiences are most commonly associated with the primary grades, big books do exist for older children, and the range of associated activities is vast. Shared reading is also a most effective strategy to use with ESL students of all ages.

In shared reading, the teacher uses a text that all students in the class can see. The text can be a commercially published or child- or teacher-authored big book, or it can be printed on chart paper, slides, or overheads. Appropriate texts can also reflect the oral and literacy traditions of the student community through songs or poetry. Likewise, they can include alternative texts of class routines, rules, labels, and directions, reinforcing the concept that reading is relevant for action.

In shared reading experiences, students learn sight words and sound–letter relationships, incidentally when the teacher points to them while reading, and directly when she or he draws attention to them for the purpose of discussion. Words students already know through speech and hearing are emphasized or noted in print by the teacher, so that they will eventually be recognized (sight words). Corresponding letter sounds are easy to remember because of the student's familiarity with the word in context and the known common sounds of several of the letters. By hearing favorite stories over and over again, by speaking, singing, or chanting them in unison, and by seeing the words and letters pointed to, children synchronize their ears, voices, and eyes with the print, leading eventually to independent reading.

Adapting the Approach of Shared Reading

Janet Allen has revisited sharing texts with older students by reading the text aloud as they follow along. Her readers' growth proved her belief that choosing the right texts for shared reading is critical to positive attitudes toward reading. Many of them were adamant that when the teacher stopped reading "good stuff," their interest in reading decreased, and when the teacher made them just read by themselves, it "was just too hard, so I stopped trying."

These students also had solid advice for us about the instruction related to shared reading. They didn't want the reading interrupted too much, but they did report enjoying and learning from instruction connected to read-alouds and shared reading in the following five categories:
1. showing what good reading sounds like
2. learning new things together
3. getting ideas for books for independent reading
4. learning new words
5. learning how to read hard texts (strategy demonstrations)

Sequential Shared Reading Activities

1. Introduce a New Story

At least once a week, introduce a new story in big-book format. The primary aim of the first reading will be to simply enjoy the story. Begin by displaying the cover and inviting the students to make predictions about it. List their predictions and talk about the author and illustrator before reading. To do a cued reading, cover the text and invite the students to make predictions of what the story is about based solely on the pictures. These predictions can be recorded and later compared to the students' understanding of the story based on hearing the words and looking at the illustrations. Reading the story with enthusiasm helps to engage the students' attention, making for lively post-reading discussions. Then read the story again.

2. Collective Rereading and Discussion

For a period of five to six days, reread and discuss one of the class' favorite rhymes, songs, poems, or stories. Point to words while reading and emphasize aspects of print and reading strategies that you want to reinforce (e.g., predicting, using context cues). Singing, choral speaking, or chanting repeated refrains is another way to involve students in shared reading. Stories with rhyme may encourage them to tap, chant, or dance. Emotion-laden words from the context of the story can be emphasized to generate a discussion and stimulate role playing to explore the words further. When finished, go back to the text and ask the students to find (read) the specific words they have discussed. A favorite activity is to have students be the words. With your help, they print the words and punctuation marks on cardboard before lining up to tell the story.

After discussions and activities stressing the meaning of the story and words, you may wish to include activities emphasizing the mechanics of language, as illustrated in the following examples:

- Begin by writing the letters of the alphabet in a row across the chalkboard. Assign one word to each student. Ask them to come up to the board and make a mark under each letter that is found in their word. When everyone has finished, count the marks under each letter and make a graph. The students can identify the most common letters.

- Have students sort the words according to length (number of letters in each word) and then match the appropriate words with corresponding cut-up numerals. Students can then sort the words according to one letter (preferably a pure initial sound). They can look at words where the letter is in the middle or end and discuss the sound it makes.

- Select and show two words with clear and different initial consonant sounds (e.g., bear, little). Have the students pronounce the words and notice the placement of their tongues and the shape of their mouths as they say the words and initial letters. What do these letters and words taste like? Brainstorm other words that start with the same letters and have the same sounds to make a key-word chart that can be added to during the year.

- Isolating particular sounds in known words helps children to remember them. With subsequent selections of the text, you may choose to focus on other sound–letter relationships, punctuation marks, or a multitude of other aspects of print.

At every opportunity, help students predict, share feelings, use approximations, rerun/correct miscues, check for meaning, confirm, elaborate, make connections, see similarities and differences, and draw conclusions about what they are reading and discussing. Conclude with a collective rereading of the story.

3. Rereading the Story Independently

This is the most important follow-up activity to the shared reading experience. Students can have a small version of a big book or individual copies of class-authored big books to read and reread. Often, the selections are available as audio recordings, or students can make their own. Listening to the recordings facilitates learning to read. Children may want to read selections from the text aloud to you, a buddy, or a broader audience. (In the case of oral reading to an audience, it is necessary for the students to want to read to a number of people and for them to have taken the time to rehearse the reading.) They can also participate, in smaller groups, in related arts, crafts, drama, music, and writing activities as additional reading response. Opportunities should be provided for children to share their responses with other groups or the class as a whole.

44. Guided Reading

Most children benefit from guided reading instruction. The guided reading lesson focuses on developing confidence, fluency, independence, and early reading strategies. Teachers need to be aware of each child's competencies, experiences, and interests. Guided reading instruction may involve the whole class or a small group.

During whole-class guided reading instruction, students read and discuss the same book at the same time. The way this is done varies: teachers may read aloud while students follow along, or teachers may ask students to read a part of the text silently for a specific purpose.

Students who are quick readers may be asked to "find the sentence that tells us... ." Individual silent reading, paired reading, or a class discussion may all be part of whole-class guided reading. Whole-class guided reading is an effective way to observe students' strategies and attitudes while building a reading community.

Small-group guided reading focuses on high-level discussion in which students react to all or part of a text, and is especially effective for teaching specific skills that require close supervision and interaction. It allows the teacher to observe strategies that the students are using and to get to know each child as a reader.

Key Elements of a Guided Reading Session

1. Group students who share a similar reading level.
2. Choose an appropriate text for the group that will lead to reading success.
3. Ask the students to sit in a circle.
4. Introduce the text by looking at its pictures (especially with emergent readers), and discuss a few potentially difficult words, the concepts, and the purpose of reading.
5. Ask students to read the text silently, if possible, and independently.
6. Observe them as they read the text. Make notes of your observations.
7. At the end of the reading, discuss the book with students – its plot, vocabulary, and concepts, and especially the reading strategies they used. Students can then take part in an extension activity, such as talking as if they were characters, or drawing the setting of the story.
8. Focus on rereading parts of the text as necessary for the discussion.
9. Draw attention to word patterns and sentence patterns to help in identifying unfamiliar words.
10. Sometimes you can cut sentences, phrases, and words from the story and have students reconstruct the text.
11. Complete a running record with one student per group.
12. Assess the students' development. Note those who need to move to another group.

Five Benefits of Guided Reading

1. Students can develop strategies that help them grow as readers, now and in the years to come.
2. Students will have the opportunity to develop both individual skills (reading) and co-operative skills (as members of a group).
3. Students can read aloud to their peers in response to having read the text, not for assessment purposes but for the pleasure of reading aloud a piece of literature that appeals to them.
4. Students are immersed in reading in a comfortable environment where their learning, their opinions, and their reactions are valued.
5. Guided reading sessions present opportunities for us, as teachers, to capitalize on teachable moments and observe students as they are reading and responding in a structured and enabling environment.

Leveling a Set of Core Books for Guided Reading

Classroom libraries can be organized in a variety of ways, and books in these libraries need not be graded. Books used for guided reading, however, must be grouped according to level of difficulty.

The most important consideration in assigning a level to a book rests on whether students at the level can read at a rate of 90–95 percent accuracy. For each level, there should be several books. If we were to organize groups in a class that were exact in terms of their reflection of students' reading abilities, we would likely end up with countless groups. Instead, we need to group students whose abilities, knowledge, and experiences are similar. For this reason, our groups will contain a range of readers, and the books we choose for them must reflect this reality. At the early reading level, these differences in text will be small. At the emergent level, differences will be greater. And they will be greater still at the developing level.

Guided reading collections can take time to build. To begin, you will likely need the help of colleagues, including the school librarian, to find copies of the same book (book sales can also be a good source). Selections of school anthologies represent another source of reading material.

45. Literature Circles

A literature circle typically comprises a group of students who are reading the same book and who come together in small heterogeneous groups to discuss, react, and share responses. The purpose of the circle is to promote reading and responses to literature through discussion and to provide opportunities for students to work in small groups. When first starting literature groups, the teacher may choose the same book for everyone to read. As time progresses, students should be encouraged to choose from among three or four books, giving them some control over their own learning.

When organizing literature circles for the first time, teachers may want to assign students to a group. However, once they become familiar with literature circles, they can form their own groups. The teacher's role is now that of observer and evaluator, problem solver and facilitator. She or he monitors the groups and may join a group to add to the discussion. When there are more than five students who want to read the same book, several groups may be formed. With chapter books, students usually meet following each reading session. Literature groups meet three times per week

for a period of fifteen to thirty minutes; the sessions can last from one day to six weeks, depending on the length of the book. Of course, the entire class does not have to be engaged in a literature group at the same time.

Literature circles may take time to establish. Introduction, explanation, and demonstration of the concept of a literature circle and good questioning and discussion behavior provide the appropriate atmosphere for success. A literature circle discussion chart can prompt and spark discussion, and may include some of the following:

- talk about the book's title and author
- discussions of what has been read
- identifying favorite parts of a book, and reasons for these choices
- listing topics for the next discussion

Before beginning to read, students may do an introductory activity. This can include answering a survey or questions, or completing a cloze activity or a "What I know about… ." Students come to the group with their reading and journal entries completed. Reading goals and other information for the next meeting should be recorded in the journals. Oral reading occurs only when a concept needs to be clarified or when beginning readers or other students need assistance – the teacher may need to read aloud to this group. As well, an audio recording of the book can be placed in the listening centre for those who need it. Students can do their silent reading in class, and discussions can follow after they have completed a small chunk of the text. Group members can decide on what to read next and how much they will cover. (Some readers-at-risk may need to listen to a recorded version as they read to prepare for the discussion.)

There are many benefits of using literature circles. Students take charge of their learning, all improve listening and comprehension skills, and those who are reading below level gain in self-esteem through participating equally with their peers. Generally, literature circles give students the opportunity to appreciate that everyone has different points of view while all have the opportunity to speak and be heard.

Journals can be used as both follow-up to the discussion and as preparation and guiding statements during the next discussion. Making a video recording of a session can help the teacher observe the dynamics of the group and the literacy behavior of its members. As well, the group can view the video after completing discussions on the book and reflect on their contributions and the process. An assessment meeting can be held to consider modifying the mode of working, and each member can self-reflect using his or her journal. This process models future shared literacy events, from discussions on work-related issues to participating in political action groups. Students talk, read, write, and think for real purposes. Such self-regulating management takes time to establish. Periodic whole-class discussions can generate guidelines to help children function and grow from the process.

Roles to Assign During Literature Circles

To help students become accustomed to participating fully in literature groups, some teachers assign roles, vary the duties, and eliminate them when they are no longer needed.

Instigator – raises issues for the group to discuss based on the day's reading

Linguist – draws group's attention to interesting words in the story (notes the page number) and discusses their meaning with the group

Literary Artist – chooses an event or mood conveyed in the reading and illustrates it for the group (can add to a collection of day's pictures)

Literary Critic – finds examples of effective use of literacy techniques in passages, and, conversely, passages that are problematic

Questioner – presents puzzling issues – relating to personal response, as well as content – raised in the day's reading for the group to consider

Reteller – summarizes the day's reading for the group

Text Enricher – supports the text by bringing in other related stories or non-fiction articles, books by the same place of during the same time period

---

46. Independent Reading

Independent reading gives students opportunities to read on their own and helps them to develop unique interests and an appreciation of the variety of literature. Focused independent reading programs require planning and commitment on the teacher's part. When independent reading is scheduled, the student can prepare by finding material of significant interest.

A reading corner provides a focus for reading, but teachers need to be aware that choice and self-directed reading cannot be isolated in a particular context. Independent selection depends on an environment that allows for opportunities of choice to be present in varied and enriched contexts. The opportunity to read is also extended through recordings students can listen to, both at home and school. Choice of texts can be personalized when recordings of books that have interested the students are made available. Of prime importance is building pleasurable experience through modeling by the teacher, as well as through personal and private reading times.

Sustained Silent Reading

A student's concentration can be extended over time, as can the level and range of reading material. When a student's sustained silent reading demonstrates developed interest in reading, the teacher has been successful in guiding the reader toward independence. To achieve this, it is important to match the child and the book in reading instruction. Reading at a level of proficiency encourages the development of positive attitudes and confidence. Many basal-reader manuals provide information on how to determine a child's reading level. It is important to teach skills at a level that permits independence and success.

Initially, short daily sustained silent-reading periods are best. A quiet time without interruption can be extended from five minutes at the kindergarten/grade-1 level to thirty minutes at the grade-8 level. Students should be encouraged to read books that are enjoyable and not overly difficult. If they are aware of their responsibilities during these periods, such as choosing appropriate materials, they are more likely to persevere with their reading.

When Young Students Read Alone

Kindergarten and first-grade teachers need to modify their programs by distributing picture books and books students have heard read aloud. They like to share books they are reading so they will need to learn how to read books silently and independently. Initially, children cannot be expected to read independently – they need encouragement and practice in class routines that will require the teacher to work with both groups and individuals. When students have internalized criteria for independent work and classroom control has been achieved, a successful sustained silent-reading program has been put in place.

Demonstrations

The independent reader becomes the owner of his or her reading and learning experience, and will be stimulated and rewarded by owning and selecting books for personal reading. A teacher needs to explain, demonstrate, and have students practise the skill of selecting books that are of an appropriate reading level and genre. Older students can be taught the "five-finger" technique that involves reading a passage of 100 words (and learning how to estimate this amount). Each time the student makes an error in reading the passage, she or he curls one finger into the palm. If, at the end of the passage, she or he has curled five or fewer fingers, the book is approximately the correct reading level. However, the student should not be forbidden to read a book that is too difficult. Some may persevere – and triumph!

Teachers can demonstrate the various levels of reading comprehension so that students will have a greater awareness of what to expect from themselves. Young students can also be made aware of the deceptive level of some books. Text, and not illustrations, is the major criterion in determining reading difficulty. High-interest, easy-reading books may be pitched at a lower level than that which children can read, but may be attractive in their content. These books are particularly appropriate for independent reading by students who have experienced difficulty – the books appeal to their interests and provide them with opportunities for successful reading experiences. Teachers must watch that students do not make a habit of choosing overly difficult books, since the amount they read will suffer, as will their self-concept and dedication to reading.

The importance of students selecting appropriate books needs to be emphasized. The independent reader may read in his or her spare time in the classroom, go to the library voluntarily, talk about books with other children, complete reading assignments promptly, and order books from paperback book clubs; however, unless the child is owner of his or her learning experience, independence as a reader remains to be developed.

Tracking Independent Readers

Independent readers can keep track of their reading, encouraging the development of focused reading habits. Reading diaries, reading records, and book reports offer formal techniques for tracking students' reading experiences. Through diaries, private or public, children develop personal response to reading and develop a sense of pride and accomplishment in reading skills, by making visible the amount of reading they have completed. Reporting on books may be accomplished creatively, either through oral or written forms, when presented in a context in which children's ideas about the book take precedence over its content. In reporting, students are encouraged to form opinions about the book – discussions may encourage such a response by eliciting audience interactions through questioning and sharing.

Teaching situations occur whenever the opportunity or occasion arises, but may be especially focused in individualized reading conferences. The conference represents an opportunity for the teacher to assess the student's learning process, and to participate in a shared activity in which assessment of the book, opinions, and perceptions serve as the topics from which evaluation is made. As in a student's oral reading, when the focus of the activity is directed to a response that is stimulating, the response and growth of the student is encouraged.

47. Tutoring a Troubled Reader

A troubled reader requires teachers who are aware of and sensitive to the many possible causes of reading difficulties, who recognize characteristics and behavior typical of such a reader, and who modify the literacy program to assist each student at risk. The job of the teacher is to help the student learn to read. There are many ways to accomplish this, but first the problems must be identified.

Teachers can work with an individual or a small group to directly or indirectly influence the literacy development of the emerging reader:

- to allow students time to prepare before sharing a book
- to develop fluency through rereading
- to establish confidence
- to present and reinforce strategies
- to focus on word skills (phonics, sight words)
- to connect reading and writing

Characteristics and Behavior of a Troubled Reader

The personality of the troubled reader may be a problem because of several factors, including age level and maturity. Children delight and learn quickly at young ages – two swim, to ride a bike – but will become easily frustrated with activities that require time to focus on small detail. This is what sets apart the troubled readers, who have a greater sense of frustration that may be combined with external pressures. Some are fearful and lack confidence, some are highly self-conscious, many are action-oriented. Regardless of the frustration, children need to learn to read and teachers can help.

Identifying the Troubled Reader

A troubled reader
- hesitates when asked to read because of past, negative experiences;
- lacks confidence as a reader and as a learner;
- has difficulty comprehending selected texts;
- has difficulty retelling a story;
- lacks knowledge of how books work and the characteristics that differentiate genres;
- may present erratic eye movements, has difficulty following a line, or rereads the same word;
- has reversals that continue into higher grades;
- displays little initiative to read;
- makes illogical substitutions when reading aloud;
- has difficulty identifying a purpose for reading;
- has difficulty writing complex sentences;
- is inconsistent in his or her reading attempts;
- has mastered only a few reading strategies;
- uses one strategy to the exclusion of all others;

- shows an unwillingness to try reading due to unsuccessful past experiences;
- shows a lack of motivation to read;
- is unable to read;
- has low self-esteem;
- has a feeling of failure around the issue of reading;
- lacks purpose in reading;
- is inexperienced with the structures of literature;
- has limited background experience and an underdeveloped sight-word vocabulary;
- has insufficient print problem-solving tools to support progress;
- may have a poor record of attendance.

Twenty Tutoring Strategies

1. Introduce new books (of high interest) and at a level that the student can read successfully.
2. With the student, explore a book before reading so that he or she is familiar with its style and content, has the opportunity to make personal connections to the text, and can make predictions based on the introduction, the cover, its title, and illustration.
3. At times, as in shared reading, read the story aloud as the student follows along with his or her copy, preparing the new reader with a general understanding of the text.
4. An at-risk reader may need to read or reread the text aloud in a on-on-one conference as you observe the strategies she or he uses. Given this knowledge, you can then extend his or her use of strategies through comments, questions, and demonstrations.
5. Demonstrate self-monitoring strategies that good readers use – thinking, predicting, sampling, confirming, self-correcting – by asking questions using prompts such as the following:
   - Does that word sound right?
   - Does it make sense in the story?
   - Skip the word and go on.
   - Does the word fit in the sentence?
   - Put in a word that makes sense.
   - Where have you seen that word before?
   - Do you know a word with the same sound in it?
   - Now what do you think it is?
   - What is the first letters? Does it help you? How will the word begin?
   - Check the word with the picture.

6. Give the student enough time to figure out the word. You can point out word patterns that will help uncover a word from the knowledge the child already possesses, write a pattern for the word on the chart, present a rhyming word, or draw his or her attention to the word on an existing label or word wall. You can promote the context of the story to encourage word identification, calling attention to incidents and events in the story that incorporate the word, or note predictable and recurring patterns.

7. Focusing on phonics with a particular word can help the student examine it carefully, notice how the letters and sounds work, make generalizations, and then restore it to the context of the text. You can follow up with related response activities that draw the student back to the text, extend understanding, increase word recognition, and foster knowledge of how words work.

8. Help the student work with the text in a variety of ways:
   • promoting discussion about what he or she has read before narrowing in on a skill follow-up
   • encouraging sight-word recognition in context by writing high-frequency words from the text on cards so that the child can match them with the text, using context, patterns, and pictures
   • creating a written innovation from the text where the student determines the pattern of the new text and the words it will contain; record his or her text on a chart for rereading; later, the student can record the words in individual booklets that can be illustrated.
   • using an unfamiliar text to observe how the student applies strategies she or he uses for daily reading and writing behaviors

9. Take a sentence from a story a student has written or has just finished reading; cut the sentence up so that each word is on a separate piece of paper. The student can use the pieces and reorganize them to make a story, checking his or her work against the original when finished.

10. Predictable, well-written literature is particularly effective with a student who has experienced reading difficulty, both at the elementary and secondary levels. It is even more effective when students choose what they read. With more motivation to read, students have a real reason to learn the skills and strategies that will help them become fluent readers.

11. An at-risk reader can benefit from reading a number of predictable texts. When comfortable with the format, the student can model it in writing to make a predictable book. He or she can illustrate the book and place it in the class library where others can read it.

12. A student can read the work of a favorite author, or work from a favorite genre. When familiar with the words, the student can use them as the basis for an original text that can be created with group members. Your role in this activity is to act as a recorder, if necessary, or as an audience. The student can prepare the sequel/story/poem/chapter in a number of formats, including as an illustrated copy, an overhead, a big book, a dialogue between characters, a monologue by the lead character, or a mime.

13. Wordless picture books are an effective literacy tool at all grades. A student can tell the story orally, write the text, have a partner write the text, or create a picture book that builds on a published story.

14. Read aloud to the student to increase vocabulary and comprehension, to introduce a range of author styles, and genres, and to model fluent reading. All children need to have books read to them, including those at the secondary level, where the experience can help clarify the meanings of challenging words and ideas.

15. In repeated readings, a student practises reading one passage repeatedly until she or he can read it fluently (this will vary from child to child and depends on the degree of fluency, as well as accuracy). The benefits of repeated readings are numerous, particularly for at-risk readers, and carry over to other texts that they have not practised, helping to increase fluency, word recognition, and comprehension.

16. We need to give a student genuine reasons for reading and we need to make the activity enjoyable. We can achieve this in part by encouraging the student to choose a passage they want to read. Texts that lend themselves to this activity include picture books, poems, and short stories.

17. When a student reads aloud to you, you can observe the strategies she or he employs. You can then discuss and model strategies that will further reading development. As well, you can use the opportunity to take a running record in a on-to-one conference. A student can read aloud to a partner who then gives feedback. Sessions should be short, between 10 to 15 minutes a day, several times a week.

18. It is important, particularly for at-risk readers, to determine an appropriate level of text difficulty. These students need to start with texts where they will be assured of success and move up gradually.

19. An at-risk reader can be a buddy reader to a younger child. The older child finds a book to read during the buddy session and practises it before reading it aloud to the younger child. The opportunity to read to another who will see them as a reader serves as a confidence builder.

20. For some students, having an audio recording of the story gives them the confidence to read it. Although there are a number of commercial tapes, DVDs, and CDs, a student can benefit from hearing your voice. You can read the text word by word at a rate that is comfortable for the student. When the student can read the text fluently, she or he can tape the story for another reader. While the focus of the activity is reading for pleasure, rereading aids fluency, and increases sight vocabulary and story comprehension.

48. Think-Alouds

When we ask a student to think aloud, or when a child thinks aloud as she or he solves a problem, we can witness – at least in part – their thinking process as they work.

Before we ask a student to think aloud, we have to establish a climate of trust, since it can be unnerving to describe to another what we are thinking. When we see a student stumble while reading, we can listen to the student describe his or her thought processes. We need to refrain from asking leading questions, for students may assume that we are looking for a particular response.

When students have finished describing how they have tried to make sense of the text, we can discuss how this particular strategy helps them to problem solve. Articulating the process helps students become aware of the strategies they have on hand, and empowers them as readers as they begin to realize they have ways to learn that they can call on when needed.

We can extend their learning by modeling aloud our own think-aloud strategies. Reading is a strategy-based activity; when students are aware of the strategies they need to read, they are more confident in their ability to tackle new text.

Part F: The Writing Workshop

49. Reasons for Writing

50. Computers in the Writing Program

51. The Writing Process

52. Writing Personal Stories

53. Patterns, Genres, and Formats for Writing

54. Information and Research

55. Writing From Our Reading

56. Shared Writing

57. Interactive Writing

58. Guided Writing

59. Ideas for Cooperative Writing Experiences

60. Notebooks

61. Writing in Role

62. Transforming Texts

63. Editing the Writing

64. Authors' Circles

65. Publishing the Writing

66. Assessing Writing

49. Reasons for Writing

Students need to use writing for purposes they feel are significant. An important component of a successful writing program is the inclusion and maintenance of predictable, regular writing times. Teachers need to familiarize students with elements of the writing process and the inherent time commitment for each stage – drafting, revising, rethinking, redrafting, editing, and publishing.

Teachers need to share their own writing with students, and encourage them to author their life histories as readers and writers. An open and accepting writing environment will offer a range of writing experiences and products, including diaries, journals, letters, surveys, how-to books, games, applications, résumés, bibliographies, autobiographies, lyrics, rhymes, riddles, headlines, articles, editorials, essays, memos, advertisements, commercials, brochures, questionnaires, petitions, dialogues, screenplays, and legends.

- Teachers can encourage children to
- write about things they know about,
- write about topics that matter most to them,
- be experts on a topic and teach others (helps children to know what they know),
- share topic ideas (good topics are contagious).

Authentic writing…

- develops decision-making skills: learners are involved in choosing their topic, their audience, and their genre.
- gives people voices in the world: writing gives an opportunity for the historian, the ecologist, the dreamer, the child to share opinions and ideas with the world.
- helps us rehearse our thoughts: it allows time for reflection and refining before we share our ideas with others.
- seeks and elicits response: written language is for reading, singing, mailing, exchanging, cooking – when writers imagine the response of their audience, it compels them to revise and improve their writing to obtain the response they seek.
- aids us in finding significance, direction, and beauty in our lives: helping children to write well can help them to live well, but to accomplish this the writing must be significant in scope and sequence.
- is self-affirming: learners need to know that what they have to say about their lives, their ideas, and their experiences is valued and worthwhile exploring and expressing. Using their experiences and memories can result in a deeper understanding of themselves and their environment. When taken beyond the classroom, this understanding can help them lead more thoughtful lives.

---

50. Computers in the Writing Program

Computers can be effective tools for writing in the classroom. They enable students to focus more on content, since the physical constraints of manual writing are reduced. They assist in the construction of substantive knowledge by helping students develop self-evaluative and meaning-level precision skills, as well as a procedural knowledge for writing (aimed at mechanics and syntax). This frees them to devote more time to generating ideas. A primary challenge for the educational system is to determine how to take advantage of this technology.

Benefits of Using Computers in the Writing Program

1. The quality and fluency of writing is increased. Students provide more details and revise more. As well, they confer with teachers more frequently, thus becoming more involved in the writing process.
2. The amount of talk about text meaning is increased, as well as error detection in peer writing. This encourages self-monitoring and introduces students to collaborative writing.
3. Some programs are specifically designed to help students develop planning processes in writing, narrative writing skills, expressive writing, and revision and editing skills.

4. Computers can be used for a variety of writing activities, including letters, stories, poems, messages, mail, newspapers, banners, book logs, and journals.
5. Along with a modem, computers can provide an authentic and interactive means for having children write to one another. Some classrooms have begun sharing journals with classes in other towns and cities, and even in other countries.
6. Teachers, like the students they teach, are discovering the usefulness of computers to share ideas and teaching tips with colleagues.

51. The Writing Process

Teachers need to engage students in their writing so that they will want to continue the writing process, which involves rethinking and revisiting their writing to develop strength or clarity, to alter its organization, or to select effective words and language structure.

Draft 1: Piecing Together

Students begin to compose during this stage of the writing process. The principal purpose of this stage is to set down their thoughts and feelings. Until they have written what they want to say, exactly as they wish to say it, students do not place much emphasis on editorial issues.

Draft 2: Self-Edit

In order to clarify and extend meaning, students self-edit their first draft.

Strong Point Check
Students place a checkmark (✓) beside strong points of their writing and then try to build on them by adding additional details and information. They star (*) weaker points, and try to make them stronger by changing words and/or sentences.

Distance
Writers benefit from leaving their writing for a day or two. When they pick it up again, they are better able to "re-see" their writing.

Captive Audience
Writers can read a draft aloud to themselves. This enables them to read while simultaneously listening to their work. After the writers have employed at least two methods of self-editing, they are ready for draft three.

Draft 3: Peer Edit

Group Share
Writers are encouraged to share their work with a group. They can reflect on their work and ask specific questions of their listeners. Feedback can take the form of suggestions, as well as questions for clarification. Teachers can facilitate group share by reserving time for it during literacy classes. Listening to the writing of their peers not only gives students fresh ideas, but is also a strong motivator.

Partner Trade-Ins
Partners can trade journals and enter written feedback on each other's writing. As well, writers can read their own compositions to a partner. The partner's job is to offer courteous and helpful feedback.

Draft 4: Teacher Edit

Regular student–teacher conferencing is necessary during the drafting process. However, the teacher should edit only after the student has finalized the text, ensuring that content takes priority over editorial issues.

Draft 5: Published Copy

Students choose an appropriate format for their writing. They incorporate all revisions, and recopy or input their final version of the text, adding illustrations if desired. When finished, they can share their work with their peers.

52. Writing Personal Stories

When personal stories are developed and shared, young authors become aware that writing is a natural process. By linking personal experiences with developing language skills, children find that their lives hold the potential for starting points of significant writing.

We need to encourage our students to tell the stories of their own lives. They can borrow the shapes and cadences, the words and phrases, of the professional authors they have read or that they have heard read aloud by generous parents and teachers. A student's identity, culture, and origins may be revealed in each story told, and the resulting experience will give the original tale a pattern and texture that will enrich both the teller and the told.

**Tips for Strengthening Students'
Story Lives**

- Make the classroom a safe place and a starting point for sharing life tales.
- Encourage spontaneous personal storytelling on each occasion when it is appropriate.
- Ask students to connect their own experiences to what they have read about or listened to.
- Use special events (a touring play, a professional storyteller, a visiting guest) as an occasion for sharing memories stimulated by the experience.
- Allow time for students to recount life stories formally during current events, or informally on rainy day recesses or at cleanup times.
- Use polished life tales as building blocks for personal writing, for painting, or inside the safety of role playing in a drama lesson.
- Help students to use real-life stories as the basis for their fiction creations, both strengthening believability of their writing and offering them a means for handling sensitive issues.
- Design opportunities for deep listening to the stories of others with a visit to a home for senior citizens or a hospice.
- Arrange for sharing stories with a buddy class of different-aged students in the school, or have a local high-school class come and tell polished life tales about their years in elementary grades.
- Tell your own life tales from both your teaching word and your personal life to strengthen or model a point that arises during a discussion or a shared reading. Swapping tales is still the best way of motivating your students to tell their stories.

Reflections

Students relax in a quiet spot, focus on something they want to clarify or think through, and let the topic fill their mind until ideas come to them (ideas can be recorded). As an alternative, they can form a small-group focus session where all concentrate on the same object. Students, who do not talk through the activity, pass a piece of paper on which each child contributes a thought.

Sharing Personal Revelations

Ask students to reread several memoir pieces to look for recurring themes or issues in their lives. For some, a writing conference can help to shape their focus and increase awareness of important personal issues. As they read, students can jot ideas, moments, and realizations central to the theme or issue to help them during the composition phase. After they have composed their first draft, they read their work to check that it reveals the theme or issue. Peer editors can help during this phase by telling the writer what they believe is the theme of the piece. Students can incorporate revisions in their next draft. Polished pieces can be displayed in the class.

Exploring a Period of Time

Encourage students to explore a phase of personal growth, moving away from focusing on a single incident. This writing differs slightly from exploring a single incident, as the students will need to organize their writing thematically rather than chronologically.

Fictional Memoirs

Fictional memoir creates a first-hand view of a person or group as witnessed by an outsider. This form of writing allows students to adopt a voice and a point of view while focusing their centre of attention elsewhere.

53. Patterns, Genres, and Formats for Writings

Writing Letters

One of the simplest things for youngsters to write is a letter to someone they know.

Writing letters helps children to develop skills in a number of areas: sharing information and ideas, practising cursive writing or computer skills, writing collaboratively, talking, planning, negotiating, spelling, and structuring sentences. Letters connect reading and writing, and home and school communities, and help teachers to be aware of students' thoughts and feelings. Letter formats can be demonstrated and placed on a chart.

E-mail has created opportunities for personal letter writing that can involve children in communicating with a variety of audiences, from children in other schools to politicians.

Writing Persuasively

Persuasion is a form of communication that attempts to change the attitudes or behaviors of others by appealing to their reasons and emotions. To speak, write, and think logically, to analyze skillfully, and to reason effectively are lifelong processes. Key elements of persuasive writing include arguments, assertiveness, critical thinking, convincing writing, the inclusion of facts, details, and logic, and well-developed opinions.

1. Formal Letter
In role as members of a small community, students can brainstorm and record reasons to save an old playground. Once the list is complete, they write a group letter to the mayor explaining the playground's importance to the community.

2. Proposal
Have students write to you about a field trip that they want to take. Their letters must persuade you that the field trip would be a beneficial experience for them.

3. Contract
Children want to play on a school team, but their parents refuse the request because they don't do their homework. In role, students must persuade their parents that they can be responsible. To win back their parents' trust, they write a contract stating that they will do homework every day after supper, in exchange for being allowed to play on the team.

Reporting and Giving Opinions

Writing reports, articles, and editorials offers young people opportunities for incorporating both information and their own personal perspectives and viewpoints into their writing projects. They can collect data and observations about issues and concerns that interest them in their school lives and in their community, and then add their own comments using their own voice. Informed opinion is the heart of an effective column, and students in the middle years are certainly ready at the drop of a hate to share their opinion on almost any topic. Sharing this type of writing often results in useful feedback, and the original ideas continue to develop and grow.

We can use these types of activities as sources for writing projects, working toward two basic goals: the need for informed opinion, and the struggle to become aware of the differences between fact and opinion. However, we can find many instances where opinion writing can be useful to developing writers: advertisements and commercials, reviews, letters, advice columns, speeches, editorials and debates. The Internet can be invaluable as a resource for examining complex issues and, of course, for providing grounds for discussing the factual validity of the information. Sharing reviews about the books the students are reading allows for critical writing and promotes new books for others to read.

Writing Narratives

Story does not necessarily mean fiction. Since children appear to write more readily when they work from life experiences, teachers can help them shape their ideas, recollections, and inventories in a variety of ways. Young authors can

- draw the characters they will be writing about, building a "life map" in pictures.
- create a story map as a plan for writing, listing the problems, events, interactions, and conclusion. As they discuss their story maps with the teacher and a peer group, they can begin to organize their ideas and focus their narratives before writing.
- select an observation or a recollection from their notebooks or journals, and begin to turn it into a story.
- pattern a story they have enjoyed by changing its frame, setting, time, plot, or ending.
- use the format of a story, fable, poem, picture book, or pop-up book to structure the telling of their story.
- write a story for a particular audience – a younger child, a child who moved away, a child ill at home.
- transcribe a story they have heard or seen, carefully restructuring the incidents.
- work with a partner – one partner writes a page and passes it to his or her partner, who writes the next page and passes it back to the first partner, and so on.

Story Forms

adventures	tall tales
life stories	sequels
parodies	legends
quests	fables
historical fiction	science fiction
retellings	comedies

Writing Scripts

Writing a script involves bringing written words to life. It is literature that speaks the words aloud. Examples of writing that incorporate scripts:

- plays
- television and radio scripts
- comic strips
- dialogue
- lyrics
- news reports
- monologues
- sermons
- conversations
- characterizations
- morning announcements

1. Interviewing Friends and Family
Have students interview friends, parents, and relatives about events they have experienced. They will need a tape recorder and a list of questions that they generate. After the interview, they can transcribe the most relevant material, leaving out the questions. They can continue to work on their transcription until their story flows smoothly. An extension of this activity is to ask students to form small groups and dramatize the stories.

2. Creating a Comic Strip
Ask students to form groups of five or six. Each group member creates one character who could be in a comic strip, drawing and naming his or her character. As a group, students make a comic strip following this plan:

- make up a story using all of the characters,
- decide what each character will do and say,
- decide what will occur in each frame,
- cooperatively draw the comic strip,
- print and draw bubbles around dialogue.

3. Interviewing Figures from the Past
In groups of eight to ten, students can choose several famous people from history. Some members will be in role as one of the famous people (they will need to read as much information as possible on the characters), while other group members will act as reporters or members of the community who might have been alive in that particular time period. They role play a press conference in which the reporters ask questions of each famous character and his or her views of issues at the time. Reporters can write an article based on one or more of the interviews.

4. Reliving an Important Moment
Ask students to describe a situation they observed that made a lasting impression on them. In their descriptions, they include specifics such as setting, character, action, mood, and the role of the characters. They can work with as many classmates as needed to improvise a scene that brings this incident to life.

Writing Poems

How to Write a Poem

1. Choose a topic that is important to you.
2. Organize your thoughts about the topic.
3. Select a form of poetry (e.g., rhyme, haiku, free verse).
4. Brainstorm and record words and phrases that relate to the topic. Do not stop writing until you run out of ideas.
5. Arrange and organize ideas that work. Delete phrases that have no power or are repetitive.
6. Write your first draft.
7. Revise and publish your poem.

1. Free Verse

This type of poem has few restrictions. There is no set line length, no rhythm patterns, and little rhyming. On the other hand, these poems do suggest rhythmical units, and break the stereotype of a poem having to rhyme.

2. Narrative Poem

A narrative poem tells a story, such as in a ballad, folk song, or rock song. It is usually organized in stanzas that include rhyme and rhythm.

3. Lyric Poetry

This type of poem conveys strong emotions and impressions. Although we tend to associate lyrics with music or songs, a lyric poem does not have to be set to music.

4. Formula Poem

This type of poem should be written with specific patterns in mind because it focuses on writing skills related to control of words, structure, and content. It can be structured using limericks or haiku.

5. Cinquain Poem

This five-line poem with syllable restrictions can be used as an introduction to haiku. The first line has two syllables, the second line four, the third line six, the fourth eight, and the last line two. The line and syllable restriction requires that words be chosen with care.

6. Haiku

Haiku is a restrictive form of poetry – three lines with seventeen syllables. The first line has five syllables, the second line seven, and the last line five. Haiku must refer to nature in some way.

7. Acrostic Poetry

Writing this type of poetry is like creating a crossword puzzle. The first step is to choose a word that represents a theme or idea. Once the theme is selected, a word or group of words must be created for each letter in the main word. Each new word or group of words must be descriptive so that it remains within the theme.

8. Rhymes

These poems, written in short stanzas, are filled with fun, rhythmic words or phrases. Students can clap, march, or tap their feet to set a rhythm. It is often helpful to follow a pattern.

54. Information and Research

Writing to inform provides the opportunity for students to work from the familiar in their lives, as they communicate information and give short narrative accounts about what they have learned. They can write about topics of interest, exploring and expanding their knowledge by asking questions, investigating, gathering information from resources, and recording ideas. In turn, they can describe, explain, and state opinions and arguments as they interpret data to reveal a critical level of cognitive development.

Forms of Informational Text

definitions	directories	instructions
recipes	manuals	atlases
dictionaries	explanations	reports
alphabet books	memos	articles
newspapers	letters	announcements
summaries	reviews	journals
TV guides		

1. Labels
Students can label photos and drawings. In addition, they can write a response or ask questions to which others respond on a notice board.

2. Webs
With students, brainstorm a topic. They can offer information they know about the topic to create a web or a chart.

3. Diagrams
Students can label diagrams and drawings. They expand the labels by recording information on use, purpose, or characteristics to give the reader additional information.

4. Calendars
Students can record facts about the weather and make predictions.

5. Lists
After discussing a topic, ask students to write a one-sentence opinion of an aspect of the topic that is supported by several facts. Place their responses under headings according to categories.

6. Maps
Students can map out an area of land that was described in a non-fiction book. They can include a key to forested areas, and mark lakes, rivers, and other topographical information.

7. Interviews
In groups, have students write questions for an interview. Each student then conducts the interview with several people, recording the results on each occasion.

8. Learning Journals
Students can detail their reading experiences by recording opinions of books they have read, observations they or the author made, experiments related to topics in a book, new facts they have learned, and problems they have experienced while reading.

9. Graphs
Students graph the results of the interviews.

10. Charts
In response to a non-fiction book, have students organize their ideas under headings related to the topic of the book.

11. Reports
Students, in small groups, choose a topic they wish to explore, and develop questions they would like answered. They investigate the topic and prepare a short report that details their findings.

12. Advertisements
Have students create posters or pamphlets advertising an issue they feel strongly about, or a presentation (e.g., play, poetry reading) they are planning to make to the rest of the class or another class in the school.

13. Newspaper Articles
Share several newspaper editorials with students. Ask them to choose one editorial and write an opinion in support of, or against, the editorial. They can find a partner who shares the same opinion. In turn, they find two students who have written an opposing viewpoint. Partners read the opposing point of view, sharing with the writers parts they found convincing.

Research Findings

Data can be collected in notebooks, or on file cards, charts, transparencies, clipboards, or sticky notes; captured on recorders, cameras, and video cameras; summarized on computer disks, photocopies, drawings, and diagrams.

Students can use the information they know about the topic to create a web or a chart. They can record their findings in a variety of formats: definitions, directories, recipes, manuals, dictionaries, explanations, alphabet books, memos, newspapers, letters, summaries, reviews, television guides, instructions, atlases, reports, articles, announcements, journals.

It is often useful to have the students reflect on their research experiences by writing about the books or other resources they have read as they prepared, or observations they made, perhaps discussing new facts they have learned or problems they had experienced while researching.

Research Resources

1. Each Other
Students can gain help from each other by sharing their initial questions with a partner or a small study group, breaking the topic into bite-sized chunks, helping with categories and headings, suggesting other resources, offering support with the presentation of the information.

2. Technology
Searching the Internet and web sites can provide a rich data back for locating information. However, the material is often unreferenced and there are unsuitable sites. With guidance, the electronic search can open up worlds of knowledge to young researchers. Appropriate software, CD-ROMs, videotapes, and films can give students access to information, often in a dramatic documentary form.

3. Interviews
Students can conduct interviews which, when recorded and then summarized or transcribed, offer primary source data to support an inquiry. Besides in-person interviews, students can conduct conversations on the phone, by e-mail, or on a chat line. Authors are not always available for interviews, but there are printed conversations available in journals or in books about writers. It may be just as significant to interview people who experienced an incident described in a novel; e.g., a man who spent his life working in a mine may have as much to say as the writer of a book about mining.

4. Off-site
First-hand research sites can include another classroom, libraries, a field-trip location such as a museum or science centre, government buildings, a theatre group, or a shopping mall.

5. Other Print Sources
Research inquiries can lead to a variety of other print resources: magazine and newspaper articles, manuals and guides, brochures and catalogues. Students will have real reasons for using references such as the encyclopedia, all types of dictionaries, the *Guinness Book of World Records*, maps and atlases, telephone directories or statistics to support and substantiate their investigation.

6. Primary Sources
Documents offer special insights for research: letters and diaries, wills, archival photos, vintage books, or land deeds and surveys, reproduced or downloaded from the Internet.

7. Non-Fiction
Students may become aware through research of the amazing variety of non-fiction books that are written on almost every topic. Using the catalogue files at the library, scanning the stacks or conducting a web search can locate resources that can lead to intensive and deep reading experiences.

8. Fiction
Fiction is also a research source when investigating an author, issue, or historical setting. Comparing picture books or novels read by group members presents a different type of data. For example, the students can map out an area of land that was described in a fiction book. They can include a key to forested area, and mark lakes, rivers, and other topographical information.

55. Writing From Our Reading

There are many ways in which students can describe, and thus express, their thoughts and opinions about a book they have read. In choosing words to describe a particular story or passage, the student's ability to think critically and make judgments is challenged and expanded. As she or he is directed to important words within a text, focus on meaning is stimulated. For example, the construction of a word collage in a response encourages the student to make multifaceted connections to the material. In considering a single, appropriate statement for a book, the student is engaged in making the meaning relevant and particular to a point of view.

The development of writing skills in conjunction with reading response also assists the student to focus on literacy values and skills. Encouraging the student's response, however, remains a priority. His or her individuality of expression and interpretation is supplemented by the guidance, encouragement, and knowledge of the enabling adult.

Methods and skills of examining the content of literature are introduced and developed in a variety of ways to sustain a student's interest, and to increase comprehension in thinking and variety in expression. Books and selections that children find memorable or significant can act as "mentor texts" for student writers, offering them ideas, formats, and styles to incorporate into their own writing

56. Shared Writing

Shared writing involves students in generating ideas for writing; for example, a language experience chart or a collaborative letter of thanks to a class visitor. For shared writing experiences, the teacher is the scribe. The teacher talks about the writing process as the students contribute their ideas to the composition of the text. The teacher discusses alternatives and takes suggestions from the children on what to write. Shared writing is writing *with* students.

During shared writing it is important to

- agree on how the purpose of the writing task will determine the structure, grammatical features, and content of the task.
- consider audience at all times.
- keep the session well-paced.
- use specific expectations which are limited in number.
- focus on working from examples of written text to explore how grammatical features are used to create particular effects.
- investigate grammatical features through activities such as transforming sentences, cloze activities, and collecting and classifying words and phrases.
- see grammatical features as options to create impact on readers, rather than as rules to create complicated sentences.
- rehearse sentences orally before writing them down, thus giving children insights into how sentences are composed.
- reread constantly and cumulatively in order to gain a flow from one sentence to another.

- encourage automatic use of basic elements such as capital letters and full stops.
- explain how decisions have been made – why one choice is preferable to another.
- use questions to seek information from the children and to consolidate and verify children's understanding.
- check for misconceptions, and direct discussion to promote action and enquiry.
- make deliberate errors from time to time in order to focus on tackling common errors or errors connected to a specific teaching objective.
- provide opportunities for children to respond by
  - offering waiting time for individual thinking
  - building in brief paired discussions
  - encouraging contributions from volunteers

57. Interactive Writing

Interactive writing is a cooperative event in which teacher and students jointly compose and write text. It involves a sharing of the pencil or pen between teacher and child. As the teacher guides a child who is writing, other students can observe and learn from the demonstration.

Not only do teacher and students share decisions about what they are going to write, they also share the duties of the scribe. The focus of interactive writing is on concepts and conventions of print, the sounds in words and how the sounds connect with letters. Students actively plan and construct the text. For the most part, students also control the writing of the text. The teacher guides this process and provides appropriate pacing, assistance, and instruction when needed.

Interactive writing demonstrates early reading strategies and how words work. Students are given the opportunity to plan and construct text. Because students generally control the writing of the text, spelling knowledge increases, as well as the ability to construct words through connecting letters, clusters of letters, and sounds. Text created in an interactive writing experience can be used for independent reading in the classroom, and thus provides a connection between reading and writing.

Interactive writing is

- negotiating the composition of texts
- collaborating in the construction of the text
- using the conventions of print
- reading and rereading texts
- searching, checking, and confirming while reading and writing

The Basic Structure of Interactive Writing

1. Establish the topic that is meaningful to the children.
2. Establish the text. Lists are established one word at a time, using a joint effort between children and teacher.
3. Consider the paper that will be used. The area for text needs to be large enough to allow for student-produced work and teacher-guided corrections.
4. Write the text. The children produce as much as they can. The teacher models, questions, and focuses attention on concepts of print and the sound of words.
5. Use alphabet charts and word walls to support letter and word recognition.
6. Encourage group responses with students forming letters in the air, whispering letters, and using silent signals.
7. There is an expectation of correctness in interactive writing. Maintain a correct model. Final text should look polished.
8. Read the text. After each word is written, read it aloud. Repetition supports the process.
9. Use the finished text. Display the text in a way that allows for continued use as a text for shared reading or independent reading.

Teaching Points Made During Interactive Writing

- letter formation and identification
- word patterns, hearing sounds in words, rhyming, syllabication, stretching, known letters
- one-to-one matching, directionality
- rewriting, writing, revising, proofreading/editing
- spacing, indenting, punctuation, use of upper and lower case letters
- sentence development, idea development, language structure

- sequencing, variety of formats, paragraph development
- high-frequency words, patterns
- rereading, using classroom resources

---

58. Guided Writing

Guided writing is an instructional procedure by which the teacher guides a group of writers through the whole writing process. This includes brainstorming, drafting, revising, and editing. These steps flow together, with the teacher moving from one step to the next, teaching specific skills as required. In guided writing workshops, the students do the writing, but are supported as needed by a teacher who provides instruction through mini-lessons and conferences.

The purpose of guided writing is to give students opportunities to expand their writing knowledge – from their name, from groups of words, and eventually from sentences. It allows students to consider audience, purpose, topic, selection of text type, etc. when planning their writing, as well as helping writers focus on conventions such as spelling, punctuation, standard usage, and handwriting. It can be a challenge for students to move from giving dictation and having the teacher write down everything the student says, to writing on his or her own. The gradual addition of successful guided writing experiences helps the transition, and can reduce the student's frustrations.

Teaching Sequence for Guided Writing

1. Plan the Lesson
The small group gathers around the teacher to receive general instructions for the writing workshop that day.

2. Present a Mini-lesson
The teacher presents a mini-lesson. Instructions, demonstrations, or writing tips are brief. The topic for the mini-lesson almost always emerges from what the teacher notices the students need to learn from observing their writing, conferencing with them, and reviewing their writing folders.

3. Write

The students get paper to write on or get out their writing folders and find a comfortable place to do their writing.

4. Conference

The teacher begins conferencing with some students, engaging them in conversation that enables the writer to move the writing forward.

5. Revision

Guided revision requires students to revisit an existing draft and make focused improvements, such as highlighting overused words and replacing them with stronger vocabulary.

6. Share

At the end of the workshop period, writing problems may be discussed. Suggestions for workshop improvements are made. Volunteers share their work, perhaps in the author's chair.

59. Ideas for Cooperative Writing Experiences

1. Create an Advertising Campaign for a School Function

Students, as a group, decide on a function to be advertised. Drawing on all members' creativity and experiences, the group selects a medium (e.g., print, radio ad) and produces a presentation for the school's staff and students.

2. Design a School Safety Handbook

A group can decide on safety issues that have relevance to their school. Group members research the issues using community, library, and municipal office libraries and resources. They write a handbook and work with school administrators to publish and distribute it throughout the school.

3. Publish a School Newspaper

A group can publish a class or school newspaper. They begin by deciding on its length and the sections to be included. Group members are assigned or volunteer for roles of writers, editors, designers, proofreaders, and so on. They prepare their pieces and compile them to make a newspaper. Depending on the scope of the paper, the group may make a copy for each person in the class, or make a copy for each class in the school.

4. Write a Script for a Small Play

Students in a group can create characters based on group personalities. They select a genre (e.g., comedy, mystery, suspense) and develop a script incorporating all of the characters. After rehearsing their script, they present their work to another group or the rest of the class.

5. Prepare for an Informative Debate

Two groups select a topic they would like to debate (e.g., smoking in public places, school uniforms vs. casual dress). Each group picks a side (*for* or *against*). If they have difficulty picking a side, a representative from each group can participate in a coin toss to determine who will have first selection. The two groups research their topic before engaging in a debate. If they like, they can appoint a judge to keep order and determine the most successful team.

6. Consumer Research Report

Students in a group can investigate how garbage leaves their home and school, and how it leaves the community. They research local recycling practices and prepare a consumer research report, which they present to another group.

7. Movie Reviews

Students in a group can interview teachers and peers to discover favorite movies. They regroup to compare and contrast findings, developing a ranking of favorites. The group shares its findings by posting a graph in the class or in the hallway.

Group Writing Tips

- In addition to a group writing folder, each member should also have a personal writing folder.
- Members keep a log of the group's progress.
- Members brainstorm and record an idea web.
- Members record ideas on index cards so they can be regrouped easily.

---

60. Notebooks

We encourage students to use notebooks to record thoughts and observations. It is most helpful if the class brainstorms a list of possible entries, adding to their own list throughout the year. These suggestions might help them get started:

- write about special events at home
- notice the unusual behaviors of your pets
- sketch the observations of happenings at school and at home
- glue in a special poem or letter
- remember moments from a holiday or camp
- list books and films you have enjoyed
- remember characters and incidents in books you have read
- write down memorable quotations
- include photos of friends and family
- retell family stories
- freeze a moment in time
- keep an idea for a story
- create a web of ideas about an interesting issue
- remember conversations with others
- get something off your mind
- work through problems
- name your worries
- record your hopes and dreams

Encouraging the Use of Notebooks

1. Allow students to choose and design their own notebooks.
2. Have students carry their notebooks throughout the day so they can jot down ideas that occur to them wherever they are. If they cannot carry their notebooks, encourage them to keep a slip of paper and a pencil handy.
3. Encourage students to look for writing moments during the regular school day (e.g., they can write about an event in gym class rather than waiting for a momentous event to occur).
4. Share examples of other people's notebooks (e.g., excerpts from *The Diary of Anne Frank*) to show the variety of styles a notebook may take. Remember that students will also have a variety of ways in which they keep notes (e.g., word lists, shorthand, sketches, charts).

5. Show students, through the work of others, how notebooks can serve as the source of a larger piece (e.g., original note compared with a final poem, essay, song, short story).
6. Have students look for recurring themes in their notes that they would like to develop further, perhaps in the form of a research project or paper, or in a fictional form such as a short story.
7. Students can form small groups to share and discuss what they have written. Once they have developed their own work, they can become classroom tutors.
8. Students can lead a discussion or give a short talk on a topic that interests them using notes they made previously.

From Notebooks to Projects

In a one-on-one individual conference, the teacher can ask these kinds of questions:

- How did you decide to write on this topic?
- What drew you to this entry in your notebook?
- Was it a hard decision?
- Do other entries relate to this subject?

Such questions help students to make connections with their writing that will take them beyond a simple retelling of an event to meaning-making in a larger framework that is central to their lives. They can "check" sections of their writing that they may want to develop further, and "star" those that hold less appeal. What a student checks or stars provides clues as to what topics or themes she or he is captured by, and can be used in a discussion of criteria the student will use to judge the work.

The teacher can hold a sample group conference with one writer in order to demonstrate the process of conferring. Students can then form small groups to hold similar conferences in which they look for themes in their own and one another's notebooks, connections between entries, and modes of writing and repeating themes that are evident in a writer's work.

Students can be asked to record what they have learned in the process of writing that could help them in future efforts, keeping track of what they decide to do as they progress with their writing. Hold a conference where students talk about the process behind their writing. If necessary, ask leading questions, including "What did all of us do? " "What did some of us do?" and "What can we learn from hearing about one another's processes?"

61. Writing in Role

Writing in role allows learners to work in a new way, fostering the development of writing in more complex modes. It offers students the chance to view themselves as writers who can control the communication medium. Examples of writing in role opportunities are

· proclamations
· speeches
· diaries
· lyrics/songs
· first-person accounts
· spy stories
· petitions
· detective stories
· monologues
· novel characters
· travelogues
· advertisements
· interviews
· biographies
· cartoons
· commentaries
· newspaper articles
· announcements
· comedy scripts

Medieval Times

The following examples of writing in role activities are structured around the theme of medieval times. In order to write in role, students will need to research this period of history – its achievements, people, dangers, growth, and development. Artistic license, a part of any writing in role activity, will come into play here as they put themselves in the place of inhabitants of the Middle Ages, or those who are revisiting it.

1. Diaries

Students imagine that they have traveled back in time to the year 1300 and have landed in a medieval town. They write an entry in their diary detailing experiences they faced that day, incorporating their research findings.

2. Detective in Role

Ask students to form groups of three or four. As a group, they must try and solve a mystery that took place in 1200. The children take on the role of detectives who find the answer to the mystery, retaining the time period as much as possible.

3. Travelogues

Allow students to assume the role of travel agents who have been asked to plan a tour of the medieval castles of Europe. They are responsible for choosing at least ten famous castles representative of the age. In addition, they must prepare detailed itineraries for their clients.

4. In Memory of…

Students research medieval times to find a person of note; for example, a politician or a legendary figure. Writing in role as a court biographer, they tell of the person's contribution to the society of the time.

5. Fashion Times

Students, in small groups, imagine themselves as clothes designers who have been asked to design outfits for both women and men that will be worn at a huge feast. They can base their designs on fashions of the time. They sketch and color their designs, and list at the bottom of each sketch the materials used to make the clothes. (The materials should be consistent with fabrics available at the time.) The work of each group can be posted so that they can share their designs.

6. Minstrel Music

Working alone or with a partner, students take on the role of a minstrel. Minstrels, who were singers or musicians, sang or recited poetry that they wrote themselves. In some instances, they would incorporate news and gossip into the lyrics so that isolated townspeople could learn of life outside their immediate area. Students can make their lyrics serious or light-hearted, mysterious or informative.

7. Serfs' Petition

In groups of four or five, students meet as serfs on a medieval fiefdom. They draw up a petition that demands better treatment for serfs, and that outlines the extent of their duties and the lacking compensation offered by the owner of the land.

62. Transforming Texts

Transforming modes of print involves taking the essence of a text (e.g., story, poem, novel) and transforming it into another form of writing or another medium (e.g., video). Such rethinking and reworking of a text, which necessitates shifting the point of view, often leads to a deeper comprehension of the material. Transforming a text is not only a follow-up activity to reading, but can also motivate children to read. (Primary/junior students are more likely to read a story that has been read aloud to them than one they have not experienced.) Assessment is made easier because transforming modes of print makes explicit a child's understanding of the material.

1. Retelling/Storytelling

Retelling is one way of transforming print. Both oral and written retellings should be encouraged because they allow students to reveal their ideas about what the story means to them. Fidelity to the original version should not be stressed; rather, encourage imaginative and personalized recreations of the story. Retelling is beneficial to both the teller and the listener because it deepens the exploration of the text for both.

2. Illustrating

Children generally enjoy drawing or painting pictures to illustrate stories they've read, heard, or written. Since this is a nonverbal form of expression, it has a wider appeal to younger children and is a useful tool for reluctant writers and ESL students. Expressing what the story means to them in this form will not be hindered by their lack of language skills. In the primary grades, illustrating could take the form of drawing a character or setting. In junior grades, students could make a diorama of a scene or draw a series of key settings and characters. Even a photo essay is possible, perhaps using other children to act out key scenes in similar settings. Of course, text can be added easily to any illustration, or the art can become the starting point for a story.

3. Other Media

Students in junior grades could videotape a version of a story. They could act it out or use animation (e.g., dolls, clay, illustrations). In addition, a text could be reworked into an audio play, a choral reading, or a reading to a musical accompaniment; it could be transformed into a musical script at advanced levels. Many computer programs give children the option of making their own slide shows, complete with narration.

"The Three Little Pigs"

Several examples of the ways in which students can transform modes of print follow. Transforming can be done as a group activity in which each group uses a different genre to tell the same story, or it can be done by students working on their own. Before beginning, it might be helpful to show children samples of writing in other forms (a newspaper or magazine would be a great place to start). The possibilities are endless.

Directions

Go north on Main Street, through the intersection, past the pile of straw on the right and the pile of sticks on the left. Turn left and drive until…
Den Drive
Woods Edge

Recipe

Mr. Wolf's Award Winning Roast Pig in Orange Sauce

60 mL (1/4) cup flour
5 mL (1/2 tsp.) each salt, pepper, paprika
45 mL (3 tbsp.) cooking oil
2 onions, chopped
60 mL (1/4 cup) vegetable broth
juice of 5 oranges
125 mL (1/2 cup) sour cream
1 little pig

Start a fire using sticks. Combine the first five ingredients in a pot…

News Report

"Good evening, here is the six o'clock news. In our top story, police have revealed that the wolf who has been terrorizing the neighborhood is near capture. Police detective Hunter O'Lupus is on the scene where the wolf is making desperate attempts to blow down a house…"

Advertisement

Open House:
Saturday, June 19 10:00 A.M – 4:00 P.M.
Phone # 555-5555
Affordable, wolf-free area
Luxury three-bedroom home
Solid brick construction

Diary Entry

Dear Diary,
I just got news of what happened to my brother and I'm so upset I can hardly write. I sure hope that mean old wolf doesn't come around here looking for a meal. They say the house came down with just one huff and one puff. I think I'll run and put shutters on all the windows right away.

Letter of Application

Dear Ms. Boss,
I am writing in response to the ad in the newspaper for bricklayers. I am a pig with a solid background in bricklaying. I once made my own house that withstood all the wolf's huffing and puffing. Please find my résumé enclosed.

Sincerely,
Pig

Invitation

You are cordially invited to attend a black-tie dinner in honor of Pig, who has graciously opened his lovely brick house to guests for the occasion.
RSVP by Saturday.

Letter

Dear Pig,
I will be visiting your home soon to eat you. I suggest you make it easy on yourself and just surrender to me now. There's no reason to ruin a perfectly nice brick house.
See You Soon,
Wolf

Autobiography

I was born in a small den near the city. My childhood was a happy one. I still remember sitting by the fire, listening to my mother tell wonderful wolf stories while my father was out hunting. It was always such a fine feast when he brought home a pig. I've never lost that taste for a fine little pig, with just a hint of garlic and a touch of thyme.

Poster

One Night Only
Come See the Spectacle
Wolf vs. Pig
Also Appearing
The Troll vs. The Three Billy Goats Gruff

63. Editing the Writing

Teachers need to help students understand that revising and editing are important and essential processes to undertake when preparing a piece of writing for publication. Many students realize the need for editing, but have difficulty revising their ideas and spotting mistakes and omissions. They require strategies to help them recognize problems and make revisions in their own work. (See BLM on page 127.)

Revising

The editing process has two elements. The first concerns content and begins when a writer has completed a first draft. The writer checks his or her work and asks questions, such as

- Is all necessary information included?
- Are there sections that are repetitive, or that stray from the topic?
- Is the information ordered logically?

Invariably the first draft of any writer – child, adult, professional – will have areas that need revision. Perhaps an important point has not been addressed or a "bridge" needs to be included to link facts. The writer can note these changes and incorporate them in the next draft.

At the second-draft stage, writers may find it helpful to have a partner read their work. Unlike the writer, the partner is not "close" to the writing and may see areas that need to be worked on more readily than the writer. Depending on the partner's assessment and the writer's own assessment of the work, she or he can then proceed to a third draft, or make small adjustments and consider the revised second draft ready for the next stage of publishing.

Learning the Writer's Craft

Students often need help in knowing what to revise, specific ideas and strategies that will make their writing more effective. We can work one-on-one with a student, or offer a mini-lesson that highlights one aspect of the writer's craft:

- finding the appropriate voice
- selecting a genre that supports the purpose for writing

- reviewing favorite boo[k] techniques
- using a variety of sente[nce] combing them where p[ossible] sentence fragments
- clarifying ideas that are
- adding important detail[s]
- showing rather than tell[ing] and events
- sequencing ideas and e[liminating] unnecessary ideas or information
- incorporating natural-sounding dialogue
- choosing a powerful lead
- having a strong conclusion
- describing the setting
- giving necessary background
- developing a character fully
- using flashbacks and flash forwards
- creating careful transitions in time and place to help the flow of the writing
- choosing an effective title
- including all necessary information
- excluding sections that are repetitive or that stray from the topic
- ordering the information logically
- making good word choices – precise nouns, strong verbs, effective adjectives and adverbs – not always the first word that flows from your pen
- replacing overused words like "nice," "said," and "a lot," and words you have repeated
- looking up synonyms for a word in a thesaurus, and using an unusual word you have discovered
- finding a rhyming word in a rhyming dictionary
- using an effective metaphor or simile

Promoting Editing in the Classroom

1. Have a variety of writing resources available in the classroom. Dictionaries, thesauruses, word games, and writings of famous authors and poets can be housed in a writing centre that children can use throughout the day.
2. Stress the aspect of an audience for published work. Students are motivated to refine and polish their work to the best of their abilities when they are preparing it for the public.
3. Make students aware that what most interests you about their writing is what they have to say, not their errors.

...s need to see themselves as ...howcasing a published piece by ...ild in the classroom at various points ...he year is a positive reinforcement for ...eir hard work.

... Write a letter home to parents about their child's progress in spelling, punctuation, and editing. Set up a parents' meeting to explain strategies they can use at home to help their child in this area.

Editing Activities

1. A Group Edit
Select a piece of draft writing that needs moderate to extensive revising. The piece can be from a student's portfolio from a previous year, or a piece of writing you have created. In small groups, students read the piece and indicate where revision is needed. When finished, groups compare their notes. Did they spot the same errors or omissions? Were their suggestions similar? If not, ask groups to take turns explaining their suggested revisions.

2. A Look at the Editing Process
Monitor students' work for an example that illustrates the various stages of the editing process. With the author's permission, display his or her drafts to illustrate the revision process to others. Students can examine the drafts and use them as a model for their own writing.

3. The Editor's Desk
This concept is based on the same idea as a newspaper office. The teacher selects one editor for every four students. The five (four, plus the editor) sit at a table and discuss the pieces of work. Each student listens to the editor and has a dialogue with him or her as the work is edited. The teacher is available to answer any questions and circulates to assure that everyone cooperates.

4. Pair-Work Editing or Peer Editing
Students choose a partner. Each takes a turn to have his or her own work edited by the partner; both discuss the reasons for the changes.

5. Editing the Teacher
Share a selection of your draft writing with students, and ask them to make suggestions for improvement. Having the chance to see that you – the teacher – need to revise your writing is beneficial, and helps them to feel less pressure to "get it right" the first time.

6. Word Doctors
This idea involves treating needy pieces of writing. Students can place their work in a cardboard box at any time; word doctors (students in the class) are always on call. More than one student can work on a piece of writing that may need editing. Word doctors write their diagnosis (comments) on the work.

7. Ordering Paragraphs
Select a well-written, short non-fiction text of four or five paragraphs. Cut and mix the paragraphs before giving them to a pair of students to order. This activity helps them to read for content, and reinforces the concept that paragraphs contain discrete chunks of information that relate to one topic. When finished, students can compare their work with the original text.

8. Run-on Paragraphs
Find a text that is approximately one page long. Type the text and run the paragraphs together. Ask students to form small groups, and give each group a copy of the run-on text. They read the text and decide where the paragraphs should be. They cut the text to make paragraphs and tape them to a piece of paper. When finished, groups can share and compare their work.

9. What Sentence?
Discuss with students how all sentences express a complete thought. Ask them to find sentences that range in length from two words to two lines, and to record one of these sentences on the board. When everyone has recorded a sentence, discuss their common aspects – sentences express a complete thought; they begin with a capital letter; and they end with a form of punctuation, whether it be an exclamation mark, a question mark, or a period.

10. Sentence Weight Reduction

Write several run-on sentences on the board to model the art of tightening in writing. Ask students to imagine that a publisher has asked them to tighten these sentences, but not to lose any of the meaning. They need sufficient time to work on the sentences before taking up the revisions in small groups. In their groups, they can explain the rationale behind their editing.

11. Where Do I Begin?

Copy a piece of text that is familiar to students. Do not include capital letters or any form of punctuation. Students, on their own or with a partner, read the text and then write it as they think it originally appeared. When everyone has finished, they can compare their work with the original text. An extension of this activity is to have them punctuate an unfamiliar text.

12. *Alot* or *A Lot*

Take two pieces of your writing that contain grammar and spelling errors and write them on transparencies. Display the pieces on an overhead and ask students to identify errors and make constructive suggestions for corrections. To model the editing process, incorporate their suggestions by crossing out, adding, and deleting information.

13. A New Reason to Read Aloud

Have students read orally a piece of writing they wish to publish. They can read their work to you, their parents, a partner, or as part of a small group. Since reading aloud is a slower process than reading silently, it helps them to spot errors in usage and structure that they might otherwise miss.

64. Authors' Circles

An authors' circle is formed after students have worked on individual pieces of writing and want to meet as a small group to receive feedback on their work prior to another phase of self-editing. Participation is voluntary, but each person, including the teacher (if she or he sits in on the circle), is expected to bring a piece of draft writing and share it with the others. Each author reads his or her piece aloud and receives peer input.

In an authors' circle, students explore meaning and think critically about their work, while other conventions (e.g., spelling, punctuation) are left for later rounds of editing. An authors' circle promotes risk-taking in a nonthreatening setting, in which writers receive clarification based on the audience's questions and comments. Writers are not obliged to incorporate all suggestions, but only to consider them in a nondefensive manner, taking notes and later deciding what to do with advice they have received.

An authors' circle helps students define and see themselves not only as distinctive, singular authors, but also as authors from the perspective of readers, and as responsible, constructive, critical responders and supporters of one another's writing. Through such real and social means of learning and authoring, literacy is facilitated; students' individual roles are expanded; and the reciprocal nature of communication within the broader and cross-curricular contexts of reading, listening, and writing is both heightened and celebrated.

65. Publishing the Writing

A writer needs to know that different audiences require different styles of writing. Publishing provides one kind of purpose and audience for the students' writing and a valid reason for revising and editing. Teachers can arrange to publish and display one piece of writing per month per student.

Ten Steps to Publishing

1. Decide why and how to publish the work.
2. Determine the audience for the work.
3. Ensure that it is polished (no spelling, grammar, or punctuation errors).
4. Decide on the number and size of pages.
5. Select a font.
6. Determine if illustrations will be included.
7. Include a title page, a dedication, and an "About the Author" section.
8. Design the cover and back cover.
9. Create an illustration or logo for the front cover.
10. Decide how the book will be bound (e.g., string, staples, rings).

Sharing Published Works

1. Publishing for Parents and Friends
Collect the best of each student's poetry and create a "Best of..." collection. Hold an evening of poetry reading that parents and friends may attend. Students can set up the room for a reading by arranging chairs, a stool for the reader, and serving refreshments. Each can read his or her contribution. An extension of this activity is to contact a seniors home to arrange a reading.

2. Publishing for Younger Children
The class can create its own book of short stories, fables, or tales for young children. As a large group, they plan the book – order of material, illustrations, chapters, cover illustration, and design. They produce the book and invite grade 1 children to attend a reading. Each student reads a section or one of the tales from the book.

3. Publishing for Peers
Students can write mystery short stories. They illustrate and bind their stories and display them at a Publishers' Corner. During silent reading, they can read one another's short stories. When finished, the display can be moved to the library where other students can read the stories.

4. Publishing for the Computer
Students can share their writing on e-mail or join networks of young writers on the Internet.

66. Assessing Writing

Student writing provides teachers with abundant material to use for assessment purposes. Pieces can be assessed individually or comparatively (e.g., a revised version with the original). Another model includes choosing a piece a student has written earlier in the year. While the teacher dictates, the student rewrites the piece.

Self-Assessment Criteria

Students will need instruction on how to select criteria, which can be based on the authors and works they enjoy reading. For younger grades, try modeling (talking out loud) your thought process through demonstrations, and provide self-evaluation checklists. At the beginning of each semester or month, consider asking the children

- What skills are you trying to learn?
- What are your best writing skills?
- What type of writing do you most enjoy?

Students can write their responses in their journal. Now and then, you can ask

- What was the hardest part about writing today?
- What did you do today that was better than yesterday?

One student wrote, "One thing I need to improve on is my handwriting. I also need to improve on what I write about, where to put punctuations, and on spelling." For older students, consider discussing and recording the elements of a good story, posting them in the classroom for reference.

Constructive Feedback

When assessing work, avoid simple judgments, (e.g., I liked your story). Instead, look for a piece's strengths and weaknesses, and provide balanced, constructive advice that relates directly to aspects of student writing. This provides them with feedback that is useful and that reinforces their knowledge of the writing craft.

Writing Conferences

Conduct frequent writing conferences with each student in your class. As well, stress the importance in growing as a writer and offer specific strategies that will assist the student in understanding the craft. (See BLM on page 128.)

Writing Workshops

Participating in creative writing workshops can supply you with new ideas to help your writing. Discussing and sharing these ideas with fellow teachers and writers can cast attention on aspects of writing that require examination. Back in the class, share these new focuses with your students.

Flexible Assessment

When examining early drafts, try to look beyond spelling and grammar errors. Students need to be encouraged to use new words to develop their reading and writing vocabulary. Using only words a student already knows will make his or her writing, while error-free, dull and lacking invention. Once a student decides that a particular piece will be published, work with him or her to emphasize the importance of correct spelling and word usage.

Part G: The Conventions of Language

67. How Language Works

Grammar, usage, punctuation, capitalization, handwriting, and spelling, when used effectively, help writers to make meaning and intent clear to the reader. Like other elements of writing, they should be treated in the context of the student's writing experience as often as possible. Demonstrations and mini-lessons are effective in highlighting specific aspects that arise.

- Language learning programs need to include
  - a focus on the many forms of writing for different purposes and audiences,
  - opportunities for constructing text, individually and in groups,
  - opportunities for deconstructing text, and analyzing and examining how language works.
- Students' attention can be directed to the many forms of writing:
  - for different purposes
  - for different audiences
- We can help students create longer, more complex sentences
  - using conjunctions,
  - using clauses.
- Students can add to sentences:
  - words
  - phrases
  - clauses
- Students can analyze the structure of different writing forms:
  - factual writing such as reports, explanations
  - fiction writing such as narrative, poetry
- Students can create sentences for specific purposes:
  - opening sentences
  - lead sentences of paragraphs
  - concluding sentences
- Students can talk about parts of speech and their functions in the text:
  - nouns, pronouns, collective nouns, etc.
  - verbs, adverbs
  - comparative and superlative adjectives
  - idioms and expressions
- Students can rework sentences:
  - substituting
  - deleting
  - adding

- Students can rearrange parts of a sentence to create a more interesting sentence:
  - rearrange words and phrases
  - rearrange parts of a sentence, such as subject and predicate
- Students can use different forms of speech:
  - direct and indirect
  - first- and third-person voice
- Students can compare a variety of usages when problems arise in language use.
- Students can discuss appropriate and inappropriate language usage by characters in books and stories.
- Students can submit examples of their writing to be used in mini-lessons or demonstrations to examine alternative usages and structures.
- Teachers can demonstrate interesting differences in language from both oral and print contexts.
- Teachers can organize investigations by having students experiment with word order or compare kinds of words that normally occur in the same place in a sentence.
- Teachers can help students observe the ways in which a change in sentence structure affects the meaning of the sentence.
- Teachers can give students practice in changing tense, using synonyms, and observing idioms in language (e.g., advertisements).
- Teachers can conduct a survey of the particular jargon of a group (e.g., teens, teachers).
- Teachers can gather a collection of "sentence misfits," examples of ineffective or incorrect language usage, from newspapers or television and create a bulletin board.
- Classes can play a variety of games, including computer games, that heighten everyone's awareness of language usage.

68. Spelling

What do you do when you need to write a word you don't know how to spell? As adults we enter the same cognitive space that children occupy most of the time. Sounding it out is a strategy that we offer most students, but there are others that we can employ; it is important that we provide and demonstrate a range of strategies for students in the classroom to use.

Spelling Strategies

- Look for patterns.
- Look for word parts.
- Write sounds in words that you know.
- Write a vowel in each word.
- Write a vowel in each syllable.
- Write the beginning of a word that you are sure of.
- Write the ending of a word that you are sure of.
- Think about words that sound the same.
- Check a book, sign, poster ,or label to see if the word is right .
- Think about the meaning of the word.
- Look for words in a personal dictionary.
- Think of a rule that helps you remember the word.
- Use a dictionary or spell-check to check spellings.
- Ask someone for help.

1. Help Students Memorize High-Frequency Words

High-frequency words are the ones that appear most often in print, and these are the words that we ask children to memorize. There is nothing wrong with this strategy, but it isn't enough. These words (e.g. a, the, and) are not actually problem words for our students. After inspecting thousands of examples of authentic writing, research has provided us with words that students most frequently misspell. It is important to rethink the lists that we are asking students to memorize.

2. Teach Students to Generalize Spelling Patterns

To memorize all the words we have to know would be impossible. Helping students predict how a word might be spelled is a useful strategy for spelling improvement. Effective word-study instruction helps students discover and then generalize key spelling rules and patterns. The amount of correct spelling in students' writing will increase as they learn linguistic principles and patterns, and apply them to their writing. We need to consider

1. Which patterns matter; which don't?
2. When should we teach patterns?
3. Which patterns should we teach first?

3. Create Conditions that Develop Students' Spelling Consciousness

Some people enjoy pointing out spelling errors in advertisements, menus, and newspapers. Paying attention to spelling details can be a good thing, and developing a degree of spelling consciousness with children is important to help them develop an ability to notice when words are spelled incorrectly.

Some students may say that learning to spell doesn't matter, since they have access to computer spell-checkers to correct their errors. Although a spell-checker can be used as a tool to help spellers, it cannot be relied on; it ignores aspects necessary to spelling, such as context. Students need to know that correct spelling does matter when others read our work because we might be judged by the way we spell. Students might be encouraged to discover spelling bloopers in published work, to distinguish between minor and major spelling errors, and to become wordhunters of spelling errors within their own work.

4. Communicate with Parents About Your Methods

Whatever methodology you choose to implement, it is essential to advise your students' parents about your spelling program. Parents need to understand and feel included in the process you are encouraging, so that they can reinforce the excitement that students are experiencing. Communicating with caregivers raises interest and invites them to engage in spelling activities at home. These activities might include playing word games, solving word puzzles, playing commercial board games, playing computer games, using flash cards for high-frequency words, and so on.

Helping Students Become Better Spellers

The more exposure students have to reading and writing, to noticing the strategies of spelling, and to a variety of spelling resources, the more they will reinforce and strengthen their mastery of spelling patterns. Research has shown that spelling is developmental; it increases and improves over time. Teachers need to keep the requirements of standard spelling in perspective, and assist students in learning to spell with a variety of strategies. Each new piece of information gained about how words work alters the students' existing perception of the whole system of spelling in English. Sometimes, students may appear to regress as they misspell words they previously knew, but they are integrating new information about words into their language competence.

Points to Consider

Students need to attend to the appearance of words and to check their encoding attempts.

- As they try to spell words, they discover the underlying rules of the spelling system.
- Learning to spell is clearly related to students' general language development.
- Children go through developmental stages in learning to spell, but not necessarily sequentially or at the same rate.
- Spelling is not just memorization; it involves discovery, categorization, and generalization. Spelling is a thinking process.
- Students learn the patterns, regularities, and unique features of spelling as they read, write, play with, and attend to words.
- Writing is the best way to learn about spelling.
- We can draw students' attention to specific patterns or groups of words to help them see a rule or generalization.
- Struggling spellers need to focus on a small amount of information at one time, especially in examining connections among words and word families.
- We need to help struggling spellers with particular strategies for learning and remembering words – patterns, families, mnemonic tricks, word walls, personal lists, computers.
- Students need to develop mechanisms for identifying and correcting errors in revisions.

Spelling Strategies

Everyone, children and adults alike, uses one or more of these three major spelling strategies.

1. Visual Memory of Spelling Patterns
Writers visualize a word in their head or write it down and judge if it "looks" correct.

2. Graphophonic or Sound–Symbol Knowledge
Writers listen to the sounds in words and then write letter patterns for those sounds based on prior knowledge.

3. Morphemic or Word Knowledge
Writers use knowledge of basic words, or parts of words, to help spell related words.

Dictionary Skills

Dictionaries and computer spell-check programs are valuable resources for literacy, especially for expanding vocabulary, but only if they are used as aids in authentic language events (e.g., checking the spelling of a word in a report, usage of a word in a poem). Many kinds of dictionaries can be found in a literacy-centred classroom (e.g., picture, primary, computer, etymological, slang, and proverb dictionaries). Multiple copies of different dictionaries are useful for students looking up word information, as they can note differences in style, content, mode of recording, and so on. Games and cooperative activities can help children to see the many uses of dictionaries in supporting their literacy learning. For example, teams can find the meaning of unknown words, or give definitions that must be matched to an unknown word.

A Common Word Bank

the	I	you	and	of	said	brother	or
a	to	he	it	was	in	sister	Ms.
his	go	my	your	away	two	school	friend
that	we	would	time	man	or	still	next
she	one	me	from	old	head	much	open
for	then	will	good	by	door	keep	has
on	little	big	any	their	before	children	hard
they	down	mother	about	here	more	give	enough
but	do	went	Mr.	saw	eat	work	wait
had	can	are	father	call	oh	king	Mrs.
at	could	come	around	turn	again	first	morning
him	when	back	want	after	play	even	find
with	did	if	don't	well	who	cry	only
up	what	now	how	think	been	try	us
all	thing	other	know	ran	may	new	three
look	so	long	right	let	stop	must	our
is	see	no	put	help	odd	grand	found
her	not	came	too	side	never	start	why
there	were	ask	got	house	eye	soon	girl
some	get	day	take	home	took	made	place
out	them	very	where	thought	people	run	under
as	like	boy	every	make	say	hand	while
be	just	an	dog	walk	tree	began	told
have	this	over	way	water	tell	gave	than

For a reproducible version of this chart, see page 129.

1. Make words available and accessible to students by supplying resources of correctly spelled words around the classroom:

   - labels and signs
   - class word banks
   - word walls
   - personal dictionaries in their writing folders
   - references (e.g., dictionaries, atlases, thesauruses)
   - word charts of common errors, theme words, and puzzles
   - key vocabulary from a story
   - content words
   - family words
   - common word patterns

2. Encourage students to write down their ideas before they stop to locate particular words, using invented spelling or initial letters and underlining the attempt for later revision.

3. Use misspellings from a first draft to help children understand patterns and their exceptions. Dealing with a few errors at a time can help a student note a misspelling and develop appropriate strategies.

4. Organize mini-lessons and demonstrations, incorporating a wall chart or an overhead projector and calling attention to spelling problems students are experiencing (e.g., doubling final consonants, adding "ing"). Approaches to solving a problem can be verbalized and visualized, and students can learn how an effective speller uses words. Puzzles and games can be incorporated to demonstrate a pattern or an exception. Theme words are not useful for teaching patterns, but are helpful when posted around the room.

5. A brief conference can help a student come to grips with a troublesome word or pattern. Peers or volunteers can assist with spelling revision.

6. Set aside a spelling time each week when students focus on learning to spell particular words and patterns chosen from their writing or from words they need help with. These should be significant words they will need to learn to use. Students can focus on about five words during each session.

7. Revise the types and use of spelling tests so that students can learn from the experience. They can choose the words they want to be tested on, older students can volunteer to assist in testing difficult words, and can discuss their problems in finding strategies for coping with misspelled words. Effective spellers learn techniques for coping through successful and helpful activities.

Syllabication Rules

Younger students can do some elementary work with syllables with activities such as clapping out words in rhymes and classifying words according to their number of syllables. Reinforcing the knowledge that words can be divided into smaller units gives students another strategy to call on when spelling.

As children mature, they begin to move away from "pure" spelling activities to focus more on syllables, stress, and etymology. To begin, they work with simple two-syllable words, such as *table* and *window*, where syllable breaks are obvious. As they develop the ability to hear syllables and divide words accordingly, they begin to identify syllables and stressed syllables in more complex words. Underlying all of these activities is etymology – the origins of words – and how words can be made by adding prefixes and suffixes.

69. Grammar and Usage

For many years, teaching specific grammar lessons to the whole class was thought to have an impact on students' writing. Research today tells us that children learn about language by using it and then by noticing how it was used. Learning when to use standard and nonstandard English depends on the context of the situation; what is required is appropriate usage rather than correct usage. We speak the way our community speaks, and to alter language patterns requires creating a positive community environment and encouraging frequent interaction with significant models: speakers, coaches, peers, and, of course, stories – listening to stories, joining in patterns and poems, storytelling, and writing.

However, it is useful for students to examine language, detecting differences in their own oral and written language forms, as well as observing the language used by authors. Students may benefit from knowing common terms, such as "verbs," when discussing how language works so that they can add knowledge about English to their language repertoire. It is important that students have common terms for shared discussion about how our language works.

Discovering How Grammar Works

Grammar can be taught as other elements of writing – in relation to students' own reading and writing experiences. Certainly, the editing process is a natural occasion to discuss grammatical structures. Other occasions can include mini-lessons and child–teacher conferences. Puzzles and games draw attention to syntactic patterns. The following strategies span a range of age levels and grammar concepts.

1. Add-a-Bit Board

This activity can increase students' knowledge of parts of speech and vocabulary and help them to use more interesting words in their writing. Begin by writing a noun on the board, for example, "snake." Ask students to describe what snakes do – for example, they hiss, slither, and slide (verbs); or how they look – for example, they are wriggly, scaly, and long (adjectives). Write each suggestion in a list. Students can record new words and their meanings, and use them in future writing activities.

2. Mix and Match Grammar Books

To make these books, students will need heavy paper, markers, a three-hole punch, and string. On strips of paper, they write sentences that include a noun, verb, adjective, and adverb. They cut out the parts of sentences and group them with others from sentences they have written. They jumble the sentence parts then organize them by placing them in a pile and using a three-hole punch. They bind each section and then bind the four sections to make a book. Students can mix and match sentences by flipping various sentence parts. An extension is to cut sentences into phrases, bind them, and flip the book to make bizarre sentences.

3. Parts-of-Speech Books

Students can make personal parts-of-speech books. As they discover the function of words, they can list them in the appropriate section with a sample sentence. For younger students, focus on nouns and verbs. Older students may also incorporate sections on other parts of speech; for example, adjectives, adverbs, and prepositions.

4. Keep It Going

The object of this game is to create a long, interesting sentence that relies only marginally on the use of "and." One student begins by giving the first word of the sentence. The next adds a word, and so on, until a sentence is formed that cannot be continued. As students become familiar with this activity, you can add further limitations; for example, only three adjectives per noun, or only two adverbs per verb. This activity provides a starting point for discussion on the parts of speech and can take an oral or written form.

5. Sentence Sense

Make numerous sets of the sixteen words shown below. Ask students to arrange as many of the words as they can in a sentence that sounds like English. When they finish, ask them to explain the rationale behind their word order. Take a class census to determine what percentage of students used various words as nouns, verbs, pronouns, and so on.

plomy	when	up	felmed
the	had	the	baslurker
morked	his	lampix	the
ciptally	and	coofed	biffles

6. Corandic

Corandic is an enurient grof with many fribs. It granks from corite, an olg that cargs like lange. Corite grinkles several other tarances, which garkers excarp by glarking the corite and starping it in tranker-clarped storbs.

This passage makes more sense than meets the eye – the grammar can be examined. Explore the sentence by asking students questions like

1. What is corandic?
2. From what does corandic grank?
3. What are the nouns in this sentence? the verbs? the pronouns? and so on.

Ask them to translate these sentences into English, substituting words where necessary. Also, they can prepare a similar exercise using their knowledge of parts of speech and word inflections. Students make up a grammatically correct sentence filled with nonsense words then trade sentences with a partner who identifies the various parts of speech.

7. Parts of Speech Cloze

Copy a passage of text that would interest most students in the class. Delete words in the passage that are the same part of speech, for example, nouns, verbs, adjectives, adverbs, or conjunctions. Ask students to form small groups, and give each group a copy of the modified passage. In their groups, they brainstorm words for each blank before deciding on the best word. They rewrite the passage with their choice of words and identify the part of speech the missing words represent. When everyone has finished, a spokesperson from each group reads aloud the new passage. How similar were the group's choices? Students can debate their choices before comparing their passage with the original.

8. MacLibs©

This computer program is patterned on Mad Libs©, a word game in which parts of speech are suggested and then implanted in a prepared text to provide incongruities when read aloud.

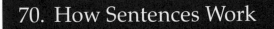

70. How Sentences Work

Building Sentences

Students learn about sentence structure by writing, reading, and discussing the language that they have constructed and read. By creating activities that promote examination of real language in context, you can help young readers and writers can add to their storehouse of literacy knowledge.

Expanding Sentences

Give students a basic sentence: "I saw a caterpillar." They can add on to the sentence, for example, "I saw a green caterpillar," and continue until the sentence can no longer be expanded. You can have group contests to see who can create the longest sentence.

Working with More Complex Sentences

For older students, run-on sentences, overuse of one sentence type, and punctuation problems can cause difficulty. Teachers can help students advance their writing abilities by making them aware of areas that need to be improved.

Mixed Up and Missing

Write down a sentence on a strip of paper. Cut out the words, mix them up, and then ask a student to unscramble the strips to make a sentence. To take the pressure off, you might suggest that she or he put the words in the order that makes the most sense while insisting that no answer is wrong. Vary the length of the sentences according to ability and grade level.

Reducing Sentences

Some may argue that taking a sentence and reducing it goes against the creative process. What this exercise does, however, is show if a student understands the point of one sentence. It also helps the student understand the difference between flowery language and precise writing, and recognize when each style is more appropriate.

Sentence Rearrangement

Give students a sentence and have them rewrite it in as many ways as possible. The one criterion is that the meaning of the sentence remain unchanged.

Story Recordings and Sentence Structure

Select a short story for which you have the audio recording and a copy of the book. Prepare a copy of the text with no punctuation marks, and give one copy to each student. Have students listen to the story. As they listen, they punctuate the text.

Comic-Strip Conversation

Give pairs of students a comic strip that has at least four panels. They convert the words in the bubbles to dialogue, using appropriate quotation marks. They add lines to "flesh out" the action of the comic strip, and include the names of characters. To help them with this activity, display a piece of text that features extensive dialogue as a model.

71. Handwriting

Handwriting used to be a component of the elementary school curriculum, but in recent years teachers have realized that students need to focus on what they are trying to say, rather than on the shape of their letters. Using a computer, we can select fonts that amaze the eye and strengthen the words. However, handwriting can help a student notice words and letters – their shape and size, their uniformity and design. Student writing can become more sophisticated as they develop control and aesthetic awareness. Often art activities enable them to notice how cursive writing can help communication.

It is important that teachers not dwell excessively on the quality of students' handwriting, but that they encourage students to focus on cursive writing as they revise their ideas and feelings. Handwriting should be readable, uniform, and aesthetically pleasing. Style grows over time with each child, but it is important to demonstrate the formation and flow of letters with mini-lessons when necessary. Practising handwriting should be kept to a minimum, but careful handwriting should be a part of each writing revision.

Tips for Teaching Handwriting

1. Use challenging, varied activities that motivate children.
2. Supply grips for students who have difficulty holding pencils.
3. Make transcription meaningful (e.g., writing invitations, creating scripts).
4. Models for transcription should be the same size as normal handwriting, and placed where the student can see the letters easily.

---

5. Various styles of handwriting are acceptable, as long as they are uniform, readable, and aesthetically pleasin

6. Help students become familiar with a handwriting repertoire in which different styles are appropriate to particular tasks (e.g., calligraphy for invitations, clear writing for instructions).

7. Make available at a writing centre a selection of utensils, including pencils, markers (fine and coarse tips), pen and ink, fine-tipped brushes, pastels, and charcoal. Students can use scrap paper for practising their writing activities.

Beginning to Print

Students should begin encoding ideas on paper as early as possible. Freed from restrictive letter formation, they will begin to notice the shape, size, and flow of writing. You can rewrite the work or use a word processor, and students can see their writing honored and yet written in a standard fashion.

Mastering Writing

As students mature, their ease with language enables them to concentrate on the mechanics of writing, of which handwriting is a component. As with younger children, teachers need to provide activities that are enjoyable and that help them master such elements of handwriting as spaces, margins, and general legibility.

1. A Survey of Handwriting

Students can explore styles of handwriting by conducting an informal survey of friends, family, and schoolmates. They can ask each respondent to sign his or her name and write a sample sentence that includes a number of letters, including ascenders and descenders. When completed, the students can compare the handwriting by charting how each letter is written.

2. Graffiti Writing

A large board and several water-soluble felt pens can serve as a class sign-in centre. At the beginning of each day, students sign in and write how they feel. When they leave, they can change their message to better reflect their feelings or leave their message as is.

3. Handwriting Analysis

Some students may be interested in discovering how people analyze handwriting. They can check the local library for information. Ask them to apply what they have learned to samples collected in the survey above, or have them conduct their own survey. Can they tell something of each respondent by his or her handwriting?

4. The Writing Is on the Wall

Challenge students to come up with sayings that refer to writing. Examples include

- written in stone
- as it was written
- written all over her (his) face
- who wrote the book

5. Practice Makes Perfect

Older students, like younger children, may want to practise their handwriting. They can place lined paper under acetate and use water-soluble markers. To make the activity more interesting, have calligraphy books on hand. Students can practise calligraphy by placing the acetate on top of the book and tracing the letters.

6. Designing a Letterhead

Students can use a computer to design personalized letterhead. Discuss with them serif and sans serif fonts, and the issue of legibility. Students can pick a font that they think would work well in a letterhead. They design their letterhead, using techniques of centring, bold, italic, and so on. You can display examples of each student's letterhead in the classroom.

7. Reading About Other "Writers"

Beverly Cleary's *Muggie Maggie* is the story of a grade-3 student who is not confident in her handwriting skills. She refuses to do cursive writing until her teacher and principal come up with a solution. Students who are experiencing frustration with their handwriting abilities may enjoy reading the story or hearing it read aloud.

8. Shape Poems

Students can record their favorite poem so that it reflects its theme. Completed shape poems can be shared with others in the class. Can they identify the theme of the poem based on its shape?

9. Handwritten Mobiles

This activity can be tied into a theme, perhaps a topic the class is studying or a book students are reading. Each student can choose favorite words in relation to the theme. Words can be decorated with found materials, paper scraps, and markers. Each word is then attached to a coat-hanger mobile. Encourage students to use bold colors in their work to make the words more visible.

10. Calligraphy

Students can begin by practising basic calligraphy (see Practice Makes Perfect) before moving to free-hand calligraphy. When ready, they can use their calligraphic skills to promote special events, such as school concerts. For small-scale work (e.g., invitations), students can use calligraphy markers. For large-scale work (e.g., posters), they can use foam brushes and paint.

11. Advertisements

Advertisements in magazines and newspapers often include handwritten examples. Students can create a "handwriting samples" bulletin board.

Part H: Organizing a Literacy Classroom

Components for Building a Literacy Program

Each teacher will need to design a literacy timetable for the reading workshop and the writing workshop that suits the particular needs of a classroom. In some cases, the teacher will combine the two areas and create an integrated literacy program. This list of components should be seen as suggestions for developing a timetable that allows for maximum literacy growth for each student.

A. The Reading Workshop

Meeting Time
- set the agenda for the day's reading events
- summarize previous day's events
- read aloud to the class
  - book talks, poems, folk tales, personal letters
- shared reading
  - big books, overhead transparencies, charts
- demonstrations
  - word charts, prepared children's oral reading
  - add to community knowledge

Group Time
- silent reading
- literature circles, response activities, literature journals (self-directed, teacher-selected)
- guided reading and/or peer directed
- organized by theme, author, or genre

Mini-Lessons
- how words work, word recognition, word games
- word histories, word sorting
- how sentences work
- how stories work

Independent Reading
- self-selected, library supported
- connect to literature circles
- assess individuals (miscue analysis, inventories)

Sharing Time
- discuss responses
- raise questions
- connect various book sets
- read aloud responses by children

B. The Writing Workshop

Meeting Time
- shared or interactive writing
  - morning messages
  - observations of class research projects
  - rules and regulations
  - experience charts
  - book evaluations
  - newsletters
- guided writing
- write aloud
  - the teacher writes and talks as she or he writes, demonstrating how writers compose and modeling the phases of writing

Guided Writing
- self-selected topics for process writing
- opportunities for mini-lessons on a variety of issues
  - choice of topic, generate ideas, plan the work
- format, revision, audience
- assist students in learning to use the revision and editing strategies through proofreading
- place the emphasis on clear, effective writing before stressing editing
- ongoing assessment with students, believing that we learn as we experiment with becoming writers

Independent Writing
- personal journals, letters, projects children choose to write on their own in writing centers

Sharing Time
- volunteers read drafts and completed works aloud
- students read published books by young authors
- group talks about issues that have been investigated and resolved (e.g., computer skills)
- publish completed drafts
  - number of times students complete a project for publishing
- – resources and materials available to children (in library, in publishing center)

C. Curriculum Connected Reading and Writing
- notebooks for social studies, health, etc.
- projects for individuals and groups in subject areas
- celebrations in which the whole class is involved, such as writing in role in a drama unit
- publishing techniques demonstrated in visual arts periods
- recording observations in science and mathematics

73. Creating Effective Learning Centres

In their book *Creating a Dynamic Classroom*, Mindy Pollishuke and Susan Schwartz provide an effective overview for developing and implementing learning centres in the classroom.

A learning centre approach involves effective management. To help you plan and implement centres consider the following questions:

- What is the name of the centre?
- What learning tasks will take place at the centre?
- What learning expectations does the centre address?
- What materials will be needed for the centre to function?
- What assessment practices will you use?
- How will you keep track of the students' work?

Planning Centres

1. Which learning centres will be permanent and easily maintained in your classroom environment throughout the year? Consider a listening centre, a reading corner, a word-study centre, a computer centre.
2. Permanent centres should promote generic learning experiences, not directly be connected to a theme or unit being studied. Consider

   - a puppet centre,
   - a dress-up centre,
   - a nature centre,
   - a science centre,
   - an invention centre,
   - a music centre,
   - a water centre,
   - a sand centre,
   - a design and technology centre, and
   - a centre for math manipulatives.

3. Establish rules, routines, and expectations for each centre. Centres help strengthen self-direction and independence.
4. A planning board offers a menu of learning centre opportunities from which students can choose. They can work at specific centres on an individual basis and form self-selected groups.

5. Establish criteria for achievement for each learning centre. Share these criteria with the students as they begin to use the centre. Review criteria as needed.

Centre Space

1. A centre need not be a physical space. Materials for a central can be stored in labeled bins, buckets, folders, or other containers. These can be carried by students to any area in the room or school, or to a designated work space.
2. Centres should have signs and labels. Prepare clear instructions for the students to follow. Ensure that materials and storage are accessible to students.
3. Involve the students in the preparation and collection of the materials.
4. Involve the students in decisions about storing materials and displaying the work.

Centre Time

1. Consider your timetable to include centres. When in the day/ in the week will you have students working at centres?
2. Using a sign-up system or schedule indicates specific times students will use the learning centres, or indicates the order of use by students.
3. Allow time for sharing after each learning centre time.

Children in Centres

1. How many students will you organize to work at a centre at any one time? Between four to six students seems to be an ideal number.
2. When exploring an integrated unit, centres should allow opportunities for small-group and individual learning experiences.
3. Some teachers invite students to use learning centres only when assigned tasks are complete. This may be a way to introduce centres. The learning centre, however, should not be perceived as an "add on," but should be an integral part of the program.
4. Consider a rotation system, whereby students move systematically through centres in set groups. This allows teachers control over *when* and *where* students will work. This also ensures

participation by all students in all centres over a period of time.

5. Tracking sheets provide a method of monitoring the student movement through centres. Students mark the appropriate place when tasks have been completed. These sheets can be kept in folders or envelopes or glued into scrapbooks or notebooks.

Centre Assessment

1. Learning centres make assessment manageable since you can focus on a small number of students at one time.
2. Observe individual and small groups of students as they work at learning centres. Record pertinent information as anecdotal notes.
3. Use tracking sheets that include self-, peer-, and teacher-assessment.
4. Observe, assess and assist students who are unable complete tasks within an acceptable time frame. A contract may be established to modify the tasks and monitor individual progress.
5. Engage the students in self-assessing the quality of their work as well as their behavior.

74. Involving Libraries

A school library functions like a hub, providing a centre for resource-based learning to students, parents, and school staff. Its design, organization, and utility reflect the philosophy and collaborative efforts of a school's professional core – teacher-librarians, teachers, and the principal. While a principal works primarily behind the scenes, teachers and teacher-librarians work together in the forefront, designing and implementing an integrated curriculum that promotes the literacy development and independent learning of each student.

Children are active learners with diverse learning styles that need to be stimulated and motivated with interesting and relevant resources. The role of libraries is ultimately for the benefit and development of the child, and therefore they must provide and utilize the most effective human, material, and physical resources possible.

Teacher-librarians maximize the library's potential effectiveness by enlisting the human resources available within the community. Through communication and interaction with consultants, social agencies, and arts organizations, teacher-librarians develop a sense of how to help teachers meet the needs of students.

Material Resources

A library must have a wide range of print material (books, magazines, periodicals, brochures, kits), media (audiotapes, CDs, videos, computer software, CD-ROMs, DVDs), and equipment (computers, television monitors, tape recorders, modems, printers, camcorders, cameras, VCRs, film projectors) available to children, school staff, and parents. The effectiveness of these material resources is determined by how they are integrated into the curriculum by teachers and teacher-librarians.

Physical Resources

The library is designed to be an inviting, safe, and exciting place in which to work and learn. When designing the library's physical space to maximize its use, the teacher-librarian needs to take into account learning and teaching styles, traffic patterns, and the number and variety of work areas needed. Consideration is also given to the availability and utility of the school's gymnasium, auditorium, playgrounds, and computer labs. Further consideration is given to integrating available physical resources beyond the school, such as public libraries, planetariums, museums, outdoor education centres, parks, community recreational facilities, and government agencies. Also, field-trip sites offer facilities, personnel, or material resources beyond the scope of the individual school.

Information-Based Learning

The role of school libraries is changing. With the development of digital technology, libraries are increasingly described as centres that provide and coordinate the sharing of all kinds of information.

The rapid changes that are taking place in information technology greatly affect the responsibilities of the teacher-librarian. The present technology provides more resources for students and enables them to acquire information from a much wider field. The teacher-librarian will need to learn how to integrate effectively and efficiently all new technology into the information center, and encourage students to become independent learners who can move freely from books to CD-ROMs, from card catalogues to the Internet, from letters to e-mail.

Literacy in the Library: Ideas

1. Book Sharing
Teacher-librarians utilize their expertise in children's literature to bring a child and a selection of books together with the intent of expanding the child's interest in, and enjoyment of, reading books. Communication with teachers and parents regarding a child's reading experience aids the teacher-librarian in bringing the most relevant and exciting reading material to the child.

2. Book Study
Teacher-librarians, in collaboration with teachers, can plan ways to expose students to new books by focusing on, for example, the works of one author, the works of one illustrator, or a theme.

Using books that represent a range of genres – fiction, non-fiction, picture books, novels, poetry – increases the potential of a student's interest and involvement in meaningful reading.

3. Promoting Books
A school library uses a variety of strategies and resources to promote books:

- props that bring stories to life
- computer-integrated book-sharing lists that may include reviews, synopses, Top Ten, or Must Read lists
- bulletin boards that display book-sharing lists
- book of the day (or week) chosen by children
- display of international stories with each story marked by a flag indicating country of origin
- multimedia displays that relate to a study unit

75. Teaching with Themes

A thematic approach to learning combines structured, sequential, and well-organized strategies, activities, children's literature, and responses to expand a particular concept. A unit is multidisciplinary and multidimensional, responsive to the interests, abilities, and needs of children, and respectful of their developing aptitudes and attitudes. In essence, this approach to learning offers children a realistic arena in which they can pursue learning, using a number of contexts and a range of materials.

Advantages of Teaching with Themes

1. Connections or relationships that exist between subjects, topics, genres, and themes can be developed naturally to extend learning opportunities across the curriculum and throughout the day.
2. Learning can be a continuous and natural activity. It is not restricted to textbooks, curriculum guidelines, or time constraints.
3. A unit allows a teacher to initiate a supportive and encouraging environment that emphasizes collaboration, cooperation, and process – not product.
4. Children's literature becomes an integral part of the curriculum.
5. Students understand that the focus of their work should be on individual problem-solving, creative-thinking, and critical-thinking processes.
6. The class, including the teacher, becomes a "community of learners."
7. Units allow for relevant, accurate assessment.
8. Through self-initiated learning activities and experiences, students have realistic, first-hand opportunities to initiate risk taking.
9. Students become active learners: they inquire and investigate connections between ideas and concepts, and reflect on their inquiries.

Steps to Developing and Implementing Units

1. Selecting the Theme
When selecting a theme, teachers can consider

- the curriculum,
- the students' interests,
- relevant issues,
- inclusion of related events (e.g., field trips).

The unit topic should be broad enough to allow for a range of research and response, but not so broad that students will have difficulty linking concepts that are related to the unit.

2. Learning Outcomes and Curricular Area
Teachers can list the attitudes, skills, and knowledge that students will gain and develop through participating in the unit, and the areas that they will work in (e.g., language arts, social studies, science, math, art, music, drama). They can decide on the most effective learning environment for the children (e.g., small groups, whole-class discussion, independent learning).

3. Resource Availability
The teacher will need to be familiar with resources (print, visual, human) that relate to the unit. Information sources include parents, people in the community, libraries, and resource centres.

4. Organizing the Unit
The teacher can list and plan activities through web charts or mind maps.

5. Brainstorming with the Class
Teachers can introduce the theme and share unit plans, discussing with students their level of previous knowledge, their interests, their attitudes, and their responses to the theme.

6. Organizing the Classroom
The classroom will need to be organized to accommodate the unit – its activities, centres, and resources. Aids, such as bulletin boards, can support theme teaching by including related materials that stimulate and motivate the students.

7. Implementing the Unit
The length of the unit will depend on the level of interest it creates, the resources, and the teacher's comfort. weekly schedules of activities and be posted that reflect each teacher's style, personal experience, and the needs of his or her students. The following represent only a sampling of schedules for units:

- for the entire day and then for several days in succession
- for several half-days
- integrated into two or more subject areas (e.g., math, science) for several days
- intermittently over the span of several weeks.

8. Monitoring the Unit
Sharing projects and activities helps students to construct meaning, build a sense of community, and take ownership for their learning. The teacher, through circulating and monitoring children's work, can facilitate problem-solving, exploration, discovery, and investigative skills. Students can be encouraged to discuss their findings, pose and answer questions about their learning, and reflect on skills. As well, teachers can help them make a connection between background and new knowledge, and reflect on their progress in relation to unit goals.

9. Evaluating and Reflecting
Discussions with students provide feedback for the unit. Was there sufficient time given? Was the topic too broad? Too narrow? How did it help the children grow? Feedback can be reflected on and incorporated when planning another unit study.

76. An Author Unit

An author unit involves the close study of a number of texts written and/or illustrated by one author. A collection of a specific author's work is experienced, discussed, and written about. In addition, students learn of the interests, experiences, and styles of authors and gain an awareness and appreciation of authors as people. As an example, an investigation of Steven Kellogg's more than 100 books allows a teacher to

from simple texts such as those found in
inkerton series, pattern books like _There Was
_ Old Woman_, and color-oriented stories like _The
Mystery of the Flying Orange Pumpkin_, to detailed
recountings of the tales of Pecos Bill, Paul Bunyan,
and Johnny Appleseed. An author study of Steven
Kellogg, then, would provide a rich source of
literature and an even more spectacular visual
display of illustrative techniques.

Materials

- a collection of books by the same author
- biographical information or reviews about the author
- films, tapes, cassettes, DVDs, and CDs of his or her work, if available

Procedures

- The teacher and/or students make a book display of the author's work in the classroom.
- The teacher displays biographical material about the author – articles, posters, or other suitable objects.
- The teacher reads the author's work to the students, or the students read on their own or as part of a small group.

Learning About an Author

1. Discussing the Author's Work
With the students, discuss the author's work, including common patterns or themes it contains; comparisons with the work of another author; the author's culture and language, and the influence of these factors on the work; and the students' personal responses to the books.

2. Responding Through Art
Students can respond to the author and his or her work through art activities. They can create murals, book jackets, bookmarks, posters, and mobiles that feature the author's work and their response to it. They can work in the style of the artist as they create their own published writings.

3. Responding Through Drama
Ask students to form small groups of four or five members. They discuss the books and decide on one of their favorite scenes. Together, they plan how to dramatize the scene through tableaux, mime, or role play. They practise their scene several times before presenting to another group.

4. Responding Through Writing
Students can respond to the author's work by writing to him or her, care of the publisher; writing about the author and his or her works in their journal; or employing some of the author's devices in a piece of their writing or illustrating.

5. Picking a Favorite
When all students in the class have read the author's work, they can form small groups based on their favorite book. They can discuss reasons why the book is their favorite and record their comments to celebrate the book. Completed projects can be displayed together.

6. Making a Historic Time Line
Students can create a decorative, historic time line that tells of an author's life. They can include events they know of his or her personal life (e.g., date and place of birth, schooling) and the dates when the author's books were published.

7. Inviting an Author to Visit
Local authors or authors visiting the area can be invited to the class or school to give readings. In advance of the author's visit, students can take part in an author study, familiarizing themselves with his or her books and style. As follow-up to the author visit, they can write thank-you letters and share their response to the reading.

Extension Ideas

1. Study more than one author at the same time, especially if the themes of their books can be linked.
2. Study authors who write in more than one genre (e.g., Eloise Greenfield).
3. Examine the relationship of an author to his or her illustrator (e.g., Robert Munsch uses different illustrators for his picture books while Paulette Bourgeois uses the same illustrator).
4. Celebrate the authors in your class – the students.

77. A Genre Study

Each genre of writing (e.g., narrative, biography, poetry, research, persuasive writing, informative) follows rules governing the format, the language patterns, and the effect on the reader.

Using a genre study in the classroom is similar to studying a theme or doing an author study. However, a genre study has many other benefits. Instead of focusing on only one concept or on a limited selection of books from one author, students will explore a type of writing, understanding the nature of the medium on the message.

Genre reading can be a helpful tool for students to explore, compare, describe, and assess types of books and various forms of writing. Understanding genre may eventually help them explore and experiment with their own writing styles and formats.

Getting Started

Teachers can begin by choosing a genre that is appropriate to a theme students are working with, or that is of interest to the class. Similar to choosing a topic for a thematic unit, the choice of a genre may arise from observations of the students' choices of books from the library. Teachers can choose a few books from this genre and read them aloud to the class, or discuss with students titles from a genre that all have read. Together, they can generate a list of similar characteristics or patterns that are found in these books. This list and the follow-up activities will motivate students to think, read critically, and become more aware of their own writing.

Teachers can set up a class library with books in the genre. Students can be encouraged to select books from this library and to bring in books of their own or from another library that they think complement the study. Teachers can discuss with students characteristics or rules of the genre in question, comparing these characteristics with other genres studied and charting similarities and differences.

Advantages of Genre Study

1. Similar to a thematic study or an author study, a genre study can be used as an organizational frame.
2. Genre study allows the teacher to explore many topics, themes, and authors.
3. Genre study incorporates a large selection of books to work with, and is therefore able to accommodate the interests, preferences, capabilities, and needs of all students in the class.
4. Students are stimulated to read other books in the same genre or by the same author.
5. Students gain appropriate language to describe, compare, and talk about books, and are more comfortable sharing their reading experiences with peers.
6. Students will be able to relate books to other books (and to other genres).
7. Understanding print structures not only helps students understand what they read, but it also helps them to organize and to think creatively about their own writing.
8. Genre study provides a meaningful context for reading and writing.

78. Grouping for Learning

Reading in groups promotes cooperation and cooperative learning. Students learn from each other, share, discuss, and make meaning. Group reading situations include a large group (whole class) or small groups using a reading series or a core book. Group reading can be organized in one of two ways.

1. Homogeneous Groups

All students in the group have similar reading ability. At the early primary level, it is important that children be taught at their instructional level. Small groups of children who have similar reading abilities can meet for twenty minutes a day to develop specific strategies and reading fluency. Further support should be given to children who, unable to read, need to learn strategies to apply to their reading efforts. Once they have mastered these skills, students should become part of a new group, which will change repeatedly throughout the year. Reforming groups eliminates the stigma associated with belonging to a lower-level group, and provides students with more interesting and positive learning experiences.

2. Heterogeneous Groups

These groups comprise students with different reading abilities and are appropriate for older grades. In heterogeneous groups, all students benefit in some way. Those who are limited readers improve their reading skills, participate more, and develop self-esteem. Advanced readers become involved in peer tutoring, which extends their own thinking and learning.

- The main purpose for working in small groups is to have students engage in high-level discussions as they respond to a story, a novel, a poem, or a curriculum-related text.
- Students will meet a variety of literature, authors, and formats that they might not choose independently.
- Students are supported in thinking critically about what they are reading or what they have read.
- Small groups allow all students to participate and be heard.
- Responses should be open-ended, conversational, and connected to the students' personal experiences.
- The group's focus should be on a reason for reading, learning how and why readers read in real-life situations – satisfaction and appreciation, information, to support personal views, to share, to expand language use.
- Teachers can help students relate and connect books and authors to their lives.
- Group members discuss their questions and insights into an author's ideas and style.
- Students can read aloud (but not one after the other) descriptive passages that they enjoyed, statements that back up a point made in a discussion, excerpts that seem confusing, or dialogue that comes to life when read orally.
- Groups are generally heterogeneous, but there may be times when a teacher will want to use a particular technique only with students who share a similar developmental stage.

- Teachers can meet with heterogeneous groups two or three times a week.
- Teachers can confer with individuals two days a week or daily.
- Teachers need to work with small groups experiencing difficulty, working on sight words, attacking new words, or reading for fluency.
- A group can complete an anthology story or a book in about a week. Selections may be grouped around a theme.
- Students can work independently on activities, some that require participation and others in which it is up to the child to decide to participate. A scheduling chart may help them organize activities, and a log can keep a student on track.

79. Conferences

Conferences enhance literacy growth, and are essential in developing "a community of readers and writers." They provide opportunities for making reading and writing development a natural part of the school day. There are several types of reading and writing conferences: child–teacher, peer, and parent–child–teacher conferences. While each has its own structure and purpose, the following general points outline reasons for holding conferences:

- to relate language learning to the student's life experiences
- to improve the student's attitude toward reading and writing
- to assess a student's reading and writing privately and to offer assistance
- to share personal interests in reading materials
- to build strategies for word recognition and comprehension
- to develop oral reading competence
- to talk about new books to groups of students
- to help a student build understanding through conversation
- to deepen a reading experience with extending discussion
- to provide a forum for questioning
- to help the student venture forth into new learning with more complex materials
- to build a literacy community incorporating students at all levels of development

Elements of Conferences

1. Comfort Level
Making a student feel comfortable is of utmost importance. She or he should feel at ease and understand and appreciate the input that the teacher has to make, realizing that his or her ideas will be respected and considered at all times.

2. Positive Setting
When creating a positive relationship, a relaxed atmosphere is necessary. The teacher can establish an area where both are comfortable. This could be a space on the rug designated for conferences that has been made cozy with pillows and functional with papers and pens.

3. Recording Conferences
Students should have the opportunity to record elements of the conference (e.g., a tip or saying they want to remember, a change in conference time). They can record notes on special conference sheets or use a "conference" pen (a pen used only for conferences). Conferences can be recorded (video or audio), primarily for the teacher's benefit, but also for the student's. If recording is not an option, the teacher should jot notes that can be transcribed and when time allows.

4. Open-Ended Conversations
Once a positive relationship and relaxed atmosphere has been established, work on writing can begin. Open-ended questions, as opposed to specific comments, are more helpful to the students' work and self-esteem, and lead to more reflective self-assessment. The teacher can begin by asking open-ended questions and prompts, such as

- Tell me about your subject. Tell me about what you are writing.
- How does the piece sound when read aloud?
- Could we compare the story/writing style with another piece?
- Are you happy with the ending? the beginning? a certain word?
- What is your favorite part? best line? funniest part? saddest part?
- How does the title fit the story? What title would work well with the story?
- What do you like or dislike about your story?
- Are there any problems you would like help with? Do you have any questions?
- Does this book remind you of your family?

5. Developing Confidence
Descriptive, nonjudgmental phrases, suggestions, and praise are necessary for the confidence that each student needs in order to develop his or her writing. Some phrases and praise that are nonjudgmental may begin

- Show me how…
- Tell me how…
- I like the way…
- The ending/the beginning/the middle…
- The colors…
- The characters…
- The story…

6. Numerous Conferences
The teacher can hold conferences with each student throughout the writing process. A sign-up sheet listing stages and names can be completed by students to ensure that the teacher and student meet at least several times throughout the project.

7. Attentive Listening
Teachers need to remember that the main point of a conference is to allow students the chance to talk – to retell their reading experiences, to describe writing difficulties, to problem solve, and to celebrate. While a teacher's input is valuable in a conference, it should not dominate it.

8. Teacher Improvements
In order to improve a conference, teachers can ask themselves these questions: How am I benefiting or learning from this conference? How can I improve? What new or different resources might be helpful? What new book can I read now? Will audio recording and analyzing a conference help me improve? When is a good opportunity to do this? Such questions result in the growth of the teacher, which in turn results in the growth of a student.

9. Flexibility
It is not always possible to have long conferences with each student. Teachers should mix short and long conferences. Some students may be at a stage at which more discussion is necessary, others may

not. Conference length can be changed according to time, stages, and students.

10. Acceptance

A student who is looking for attention or unable to focus on his or her own work may accompany the teacher on different conferences to take minutes of the meeting. The recording aspect makes him or her feel worthwhile at the same time that the child may gain from repeated exposures to conferences and the teacher's attitude toward reading and writing.

Conferencing One-on-One

Child–teacher conferences are a vital link in promoting a lifelong passion for reading and literature. Teachers must model for children a love of reading that is nurtured on a daily basis so that they can see the value of reading and the importance it can play in their life.

Through the use of child–teacher conferences, students are encouraged to extend their exploration of a text, and teachers can assess and evaluate their progress. In addition, the accepting attitude of the teacher during the conference does much to promote the sharing aspect of reading, encouraging students to become part of a "community of readers."

These conferences give students varied and frequent opportunities to talk about books they have read. The conferences should always occur in a relaxed atmosphere where the students feel secure and comfortable in expressing their feelings about what they have read. During these conferences, teachers can

- listen to a student talk about personal interests, attitudes, and purposes for reading;
- ask questions to promote the student's exploration of the text;
- identify reading strategies the student uses;
- determine the student's comprehension of what she or he has read;
- expand on a student's oral reading competence;
- activate the student's thinking;
- foster the use of more efficient reading strategies;
- recommend other books of a similar theme;
- draw a student's attention to books that present contrasting themes or views;
- recommend other books by the same author;

- promote related forms of writing;
- suggest further response activities (e.g., drama);
- advocate further research;
- encourage the student's own writing;
- assess a student's reading competence.

80. Teaching Demonstrations

Demonstrations, which can happen at any time during the school day, are conscious, explicit attempts to show students how something is done. Demonstrations can have a powerful and lasting effect on the learner, but it is the implicit aspect that explains their richness and importance. Teachers can unknowingly give negative demonstrations to children in a variety of ways: reading is a serious business; there is only one interpretation – the teacher's; students are not smart enough to choose their own texts; reading is always followed by a test; teachers talk a lot about literature, but they don't read much of it; reading is a waste of class time. In contrast, how often do students see their teacher captivated by what they are reading? Classrooms need to be filled with relevant and functional literary demonstrations.

Elements of Successful Demonstrations

1. Explicit demonstrations need to be demonstrations of language "wholes" (i.e., all the pieces must fit) rather than isolated, unrelated bits of language.
2. Demonstrations need to be continually repeated. Since demonstrations are larger, more general, and more contextual than mini-lessons, students can learn something new again and again from the same demonstration.
3. There is no set length for a demonstration. Students will generally take from a demonstration whatever they find interesting or relevant to their learning needs.
4. Demonstrations should be contextually relevant and therefore appropriate to the literary task the child is trying to complete. Students will engage with a demonstration if they have a need for what you are showing them.

106

5. Part of an ongoing series of demonstrations is the reading expectations you have of your students. Expect them to read, discover books they love, find satisfaction in books, and learn.
6. Know enough about reading literacy to be able to present a range and variety of demonstrations that will enable learners to get all the pieces they need to become fully literate.
7. Demonstrations are more effective when delivered to smaller groups.
8. A good form of demonstration is the think-aloud. Reading the text and then reflecting out loud on what you have read shows children that adults also need support and time to reflect. This is a good way to give students a variety of strategies and ways to approach a text. The goal is to develop in students the methods and habits used by good readers to become self-monitoring and independent, and able to read with depth and meaning.
9. Following a demonstration, give students the opportunity to model the behavior.

Goals for Teaching Demonstrations

- We need to understand and appreciate the developing characteristics and behaviors of individual students in the middle years in our classrooms.
- We need to strive to create in school a literacy community for our students that connects to their homes and to their outside worlds, so that we can support them in becoming independent, lifelong readers and writers.
- We need to help our students move toward becoming responsible for their own learning, capable of making choices and taking action, and able to handle some of the challenges and problems in their lives.
- We need to model literacy by sharing experiences from our own lives as readers and writers, and by demonstrating techniques and strategies for our students so that they can grow as literate beings.
- We need to provide our students with a wide variety of resources that they want to read, and at different reading levels that they can read.
- We need to encourage our students to connect the texts they read to their personal experiences, to their feelings, and to past and present world events.
- We need to develop authentic reasons for having our students write, so they will have opportunities to write for a variety of functions and for different audiences.
- We need to provide explicit instruction in reading and writing, so that all our students can acquire the strategies that will help them to read and write more complex and meaningful texts.
- We need to support our students in their reading and writing in a variety of genres and text structures found across the curriculum.
- We need to develop assessment strategies and use evaluation procedures that enable our students to recognize their strengths and uncover their problems, so that we can design useful instruction for supporting their literacy growth.
- We need to continue to grow as professionals in our teaching: questioning and reflecting upon our own practice as well as the policies and the curricula we follow; reading about the classroom discoveries of other educators in new books and journal articles; attending in-service sessions and conferences as both leaders and participants; and living our lives as involved and participating readers and writers.
- We need to talk about the reading in our students' lives, so that we can find out what they think about their reading: their questions, reactions, interpretations, opinions, inferences, arguments, and celebrations.
- If we belong to a book club, we can share some of the proceedings with our students:
  - How are the books selected?
  - Who decides what we will talk about?
  - When do we find time to read the books?
  - How do we make sense of the books we are reading?
  - How do we notice our own use of the reading strategies?
- If we are taking a course ourselves, we can show our students the texts and articles we are using, revealing our own modes of sorting, marking, or highlighting texts.
- We need to model how we think when we read real texts so that students see inside the process of understanding how print works

81. Mini-Lessons

A mini-lesson is a brief, focused lesson that allows teachers to demonstrate or teach a specific skill or idea in a short, purposeful way. Reading, writing, or thinking strategies can all be demonstrated using mini-lessons, which are often generated by the needs of the students. As well, mini-lessons can be used to review classroom procedures, to show ways to think about what one has read, and to teach specific reading skills.

A good, powerful mini-lesson should be short, specific, and relevant to what students are doing so that it will "stick" (particularly if they can immediately put to use the skill or strategy). The question–answer method should be avoided when giving mini-lessons, as it can slow the lesson and detract from the teaching of the skill or concept. Instead, students can save their questions for the end, when questions asked and participation levels can be indicators of their depth of understanding of the concept.

Introduce the concept of mini-lessons early in the year by letting students know the behavior expected of them (e.g., where do they meet for mini-lessons?). Keep in mind that content mini-lessons are most effective when delivered to small groups or an individual student. For mini-lessons dealing with topics that they will refer to repeatedly (e.g., punctuation), teach the mini-lesson using chart paper. When completed, it can be hung together with related charts and displayed on the walls for reference.

Mini-lessons can be conducted on any number of topics:

- an author
- a genre
- a poem
- a short story
- an opening chapter or an opening sentence
- writing styles
- reading aloud, reading for speed, skimming, or scanning
- rereading, abandoning a book
- reading workshops
- favorite authors, favorite books
- finding good books
- keeping a reading journal
- how to talk about what you read
- using a library
- characters, plot, theme, time, or setting
- point of view
- narrative voice, dialogue
- prologues, epilogues, sequels
- how books are published, copyright
- screenplays adapted from a book, "novelization" of screenplays
- rhythm/sound, rhyme, imagery, or sequence

82. Setting Up a Portfolio Program

Portfolio assessment has received attention as a powerful means for encouraging students to become aware of their learning. Portfolio programs have been identified with "authentic" assessment since they provide for a fluid, ongoing, and collaborative perspective on student performance. A portfolio program can

- encourage self-directed learning: through ongoing engagement with their portfolios and a teacher's guidance, students can develop self-assessment and goal-setting skills.
- be an authentic source of motivation: the teacher and students can see and appreciate the continuity and growth in their skills over time. Students review their effort, progress, and achievement.
- contribute to students' self-esteem by providing each with a "self-portrait" of themselves as learners
- create momentum in programs: as students compile their portfolios, they each create their own resource, as well as a record of their ideas, accomplishments, and aspirations.
- emphasize a natural integration of the curriculum: as portfolios grow, they will form a personal synthesis of their reading, writing, and life experience.
- provide insight on students' lives: teachers have access to an authentic record of each student's interests, thoughts, feelings, backgrounds, abilities, and needs.
- enable and inspire individualized observation, reflection, and instruction.
- be a valuable resource for developing and assessing programs, preparing reports, partici-

pating in parent interviews, and taking part in division and school planning.

1. Set General Parameters

Parameters should be based on the basis of aims, resources, and age of children. Portfolios can be

- assessed and/or evaluated,
- used at any grade level,
- a repository for "best work," or a broader collection of artifacts,
- used in one or more curricular areas (e.g., writing folder, literacy portfolio),
- used for varying lengths of time (e.g., throughout a unit, a year).

For example, a literacy portfolio, consistent with a year-long reading and writing workshop program, is

- a personal collection of diverse materials that reflect an individual's literacy development (i.e., their engagement with language through thinking, reading, and writing over time)
- a student-owned vehicle for pursuing and experimenting with individual interests and expression
- a record of process (i.e., a work-in-progress, not just finished, "best" work)
- a performance assessment tool (not a basis for product evaluation): the student and teacher collaborate in conference to identify and assess strengths and needs, and to help set goals for the learner and the teacher's programming.
- a teaching tool: collaborative portfolio assessment (student, teacher, peer) develops students' abilities to critically reflect on their reading and writing habits, skills, and goals.

2. List Portfolio Items

List items students will include in their portfolios and provide examples of optional items. Portfolios can contain

- drawings, pictures, photos and/or descriptions of favorite things, places, people,
- letters (e.g., to authors, people in books, heroes)
- reading responses (assigned work, journal entries, notes made outside the classroom)
- drafts and final versions of writing (both assigned and free writing)

- unfinished writing
- journal entries (e.g., "What I think," personal, reading journals)
- notes on ideas, observations, experiences, interests, sources to look for
- audio- and videotapes, computer disks
- a table of contents (encourages students to organize their entries)
- captions on each entry describing why the student selected it
- reading and writing logs, including the title, author, date, and comments
- memorable quotes from reading,
- an "I want to read" list of books to access
- a list of interesting words encountered in reading, other media, conversation
- an About the Author piece (consider as a preliminary portfolio activity)
- comments from peers and teacher, conference notes
- anything that the student wants to share from school, home, or elsewhere and that reflects him or her as a speaker, listener, reader, writer, storyteller, actor, poet, person!

3. Design Forms

Portfolios require a number of standard forms, for teacher and student use, including a reading log form, conference reflection form, self-assessment form, and a peer evaluation form.

4. Schedule

Be sure to build in ample time. Portfolio assessment is labor- and time-intensive. Once a teacher has invested time in design and implementation, she or he must provide time for maintenance to reap returns. Teachers will need to allot time for

- independent student interaction with portfolios: organizing materials, keeping records (e.g., reading logs), selecting and captioning entries, reviewing contents
- peer interaction: formal, informal sharing of portfolios
- child–teacher conferencing: ideally, the teacher will conference with each child at least four times during the year to review portfolio con-

tents, discuss growth, and set goals for further development.

5. Model

Prepare and share a model portfolio with students. When teachers provide a concrete example for students, they help them to embark confidently and enthusiastically on a portfolio program. A teacher who uses his or her material and models reflecting on and sharing a portfolio's contents helps students see how their portfolios could be used.

6. Encourage Students' Ownership of Portfolios

Teachers can provide a variety of examples of what portfolio holders can look like and encourage students to be creative when decorating them (consider storage options when modeling sizes). How students organize the portfolios, however, must be their choice. While they will need some guidelines and input from the teacher regarding content, students will control the selection of items to be included in their portfolio.

7. Integrate Into Instruction

Portfolios are a rich resource that teachers can use as references for activities and lessons (e.g., "Look in your portfolio to see if you have an example of…"). As a program evolves, teachers can address common needs among students that have been identified when discussing their portfolios or through lessons or activities, and can continue to provide models for objectives (e.g. "Here's what a peer-edited piece might look like").

8. Portfolio Conferences

Portfolio conferencing can take place between a teacher and student, between peers, or between a parent and child. Of these, teacher–child conferences are essential, peer conferences are desirable (depending on the age of the students), and child-led parent conferences are recommended. A teacher's one-on-one conferencing with students is essential for the development of self-assessment skills and should precede (i.e.,

provide a basis for) peer and parent conferencing. When a teacher has conferenced once with every student, the class may be ready to begin peer conferencing. Ongoing teacher–child conferences and peer conferences may culminate in child-led parent conferences at the end of the year.

Parents must be prepared so that they can participate in, and respond meaningfully to, their child's presentation. To facilitate this, teachers can send home a letter with guidelines or, better yet, discuss the process with parents in advance (e.g., at the previous reporting interview). During the child-led parent conference, the teacher serves as a "resource person": she or he observes and supplies input only when requested to do so. Teachers who have experience in holding child–parent conferences have found that they need a time period of at least twenty minutes to a half-hour, and that up to four child-led parent conferences can be held at the same time.

83. Assessment and Evaluation

Assessment and evaluation, essential responsibilities of every teacher, are used routinely each day. Teachers assess and evaluate in order to

- determine what a student or group of students know, how they learn best, and their capabilities and needs;
- maintain records of students' needs, developing and modifying programs to be effective;
- collect a broad variety of indicators that track student progress and achievement.

Assessment

Assessment is an ongoing process of gathering and recording information about, and observations of, students' performances. Information gathered through assessment includes

- anecdotal records (e.g., observations pertaining to behavior, notes on their reading),
- tracking records (e.g., efforts, needs, improvements, participation),

- process items (e.g., drafts of a written work, conference notes, self-reports of group participation),
- end products (e.g., completed worksheets, stories, research projects).

Assessment involves a number of strategies:

inquiry:	verbal communications with students (e.g., reading interviews, conferencing)
observation:	anecdotal records of student behaviors, attitudes, comments, and participation
analysis:	scrutinizing records to identify a student's strengths, needs, and progress,
testing:	intentional situations designed to provide material for evaluation.

Assessment requires

- teachers as the principal recorders of student behavior and work;
- students as self-assessors and record keepers (e.g., conference participants, reading logs, portfolios);
- peers as peer editors, conference participants, co-assessors of group processes;
- parents as valuable resources of information, insights, and observations about children.

Though initially focused on students, assessment material also reflects the students progress and success: assessment should provide feedback for a teacher's program planning and design.

Evaluation

Evaluation is the making of value judgments about student achievements based on materials gathered through assessment. For example, evaluation involves the grading of submitted or presented products on the basis of a rubric of criteria. Evaluation reflects not only the students' achievements, but also to the degree of success of teaching strategies. As with assessment, evaluation should provide feedback for programming.

Uses of Assessment and Evaluation

Diagnostic assessment and evaluation takes place at the beginning of the year or unit in order to assess student skills and knowledge. Information will be used to determine a student's or group of students' status regarding a part of the curriculum or placement of individuals in learning groups and programs. Examples of formal diagnostic assessment and evaluation are cloze procedure and miscue analysis; examples of informal diagnostic assessment and evaluation are reading interviews and one-on-one oral reading observations.

Formative assessment and evaluation is ongoing throughout the year or unit. It provides continuous information about learners' development, and can be used as a resource for program planning and modification. Examples of formal formative assessment and evaluation include teacher-made tests; examples of informal formative assessment and evaluation include anecdotal records, inventories, surveys, checklists, observation guides, portfolios, writing folders, conferencing, audio and video recording, and student self-assessment.

Summative assessment and evaluation occurs at the end of the year or unit, and involves conferencing, analysis, grading, and reporting. Results can serve as feedback for program evaluation. Examples of formal summative assessment and evaluation include norm-referenced and criterion-referenced tests; an example of informal summative assessment and evaluation includes feedback to program

84. How to Choose Resources

Teachers need to carefully choose and organize reading resources for classroom collections. They must

- get these resources in place and understand how to use them as part of a reading program
- develop strategies that will enable them to prepare lessons for different types of reading groups and independent reading times
- be aware of troubled readers in hopes of involving them in an effective reading program
- be aware of methods of teaching reading and keeping detailed anecdotal records.

Five Ways to Organize Classroom Book Collections

1. Multiple Copies of Collections of Stories

Anthologies and readers contain a number of pieces of literature that are housed together based on their shared reading level and/or theme. Those published for the educational market can be used for individual and group work, and can provide a good opportunity for reinforcing stage- or level-appropriate reading skills. Typically, these anthologies will consist of five to ten copies of books at each level, making it possible for groups of students to have a shared reading experience that the teacher can monitor.

2. Multiple Copies of a Single Story

These can range in length from the shortest short story to a longer novel form. Many teachers include multiple copies of novels in class sets, in order to accommodate the enthusiasm of young children for their favorite books. Often they want, and need, to talk to peers about books that they are reading – a resourceful teacher will be able to provide those books on demand as the need arises. Many schools find that five to ten copies of single works can be shared among classes.

3. Works Written and/or Illustrated by One Author

Collections often take the form of an organized author study – an investigation of authoring skills and styles by one author and/or illustrator. Some popular authors write for a range of age and interest levels – the study of such an author will give the teacher the opportunity to provide literature for all levels of reader in his or her program.

4. Individual Literature Pieces

Many of today's classroom libraries include a number of books that do not share a common theme. Such a collection helps to create a good environment for a "pick and read" program, a necessary part of an individualized reading program.

5. Literature Pieces that Share a Common Theme

By considering differences and similarities in books that share a common theme, students can investigate aspects of culture, social-science topics, countries of origin, or other universal themes. A good story can cross the curriculum – a "set of books" can launch an investigation that will result in students introducing additional resources into the classroom to share with classmates. If they are given opportunities to assume ownership of the learning process by finding and bringing material to class, the reading program will grow and flourish.

How Using the Same Text Can Be Beneficial

- An important teaching objective is to create a community of readers. Assisting students with selecting suitable reading materials that can be shared is crucial as they develop as readers, thinkers, and explorers.
- In most patterned or repetitive texts, the stories lend themselves to patterning. The text then becomes a skeleton or taking-off point for additional learning by the students.
- Reading the same text helps to set the stage for young readers to achieve the skills they will require in becoming independent readers.

How Using Different Texts Can Be Beneficial

- An environment that includes a variety of texts, authors, and writing styles creates an atmosphere in which, as a community of readers, we share information in a meaningful way.
- Using a variety of texts encourages students to explore, in cooperative group settings, the many elements of a theme.
- Exposure to a number of texts enables students to connect literature to their lives, and provides opportunities for critical thinking.
- Reading a variety of texts gives students the chance to learn and teach others.
- During silent reading times, sometimes referred to as DEAR (Drop Everything And Read), students are encouraged to read for enjoyment and satisfaction, exploring books individually.

Appendix 1: Black-Line Masters

A Checklist for Literacy Learning

Dolch Basic Sight Vocabulary

The First 200 Instant Words

Suggestions for Students on Keeping Reading
  Journals

Graphic Organizer: Plot Organizer

Graphic Organizer: Mind Mapping Chart

Graphic Organizer: Fact and Opinion

Graphic Organizer: Prediction Chart

Graphic Organizer: 5-Ws

Graphic Organizer: K–W–L Chart

Graphic Organizer: K–W–L Sequence Chart

Graphic Organizer: Story Mapping Pyramid

An Editing Checklist

Prompts to Use in Writing Conferences

A Common Word Bank

A Checklist for Literacy Learning

Reading

Do the students
- ❏ observe the teacher in "think-aloud" demonstrations of literacy strategies?
- ❏ participate in a variety of reading/listening experiences each day?
- ❏ read a variety of genres in different formats?
- ❏ learn to choose books independently and appropriately?
- ❏ read silently for an intensive and sustained period each day?
- ❏ read common texts with other group members?
- ❏ reflect on and respond to what was read?
- ❏ have conversations with classmates and the teacher about what was read?
- ❏ keep a reading journal for recording books and responses?
- ❏ become familiar with a variety of authors and illustrators?
- ❏ read critically, being mindful and thoughtful of the connections they are making?
- ❏ continue to expand their repertoire of reading strategies?
- ❏ use technology for communicating and researching information?
- ❏ extend their sight-word vocabularies, and develop strategies for recognizing difficult or unfamiliar words?
- ❏ apply their knowledge of reading in all subject areas?
- ❏ participate in a variety of read-aloud activities, including shared reading and community reading, to promote fluency?
- ❏ see themselves as successful readers in the literacy community?

Writing

Do the students
- ❏ observe the teacher "thinking aloud" while constructing texts in demonstration lessons?
- ❏ keep a writer's notebook and gather and collect observations and ideas for future writing projects?
- ❏ write each day for a variety of purposes?
- ❏ write in a variety of genres?
- ❏ record their own feelings, experiences, and ideas?
- ❏ choose their own topics with guidance for writing projects?
- ❏ use different formats for different projects?
- ❏ learn about the craft of writing from noticing how professional authors work?
- ❏ develop the skills of revision and editing?
- ❏ participate in guided and interactive writing sessions?
- ❏ learn more about how words and sentences work?
- ❏ participate in conferences with the teacher and other students?
- ❏ share their writing with classmates and listen to and read their work?
- ❏ use writing as a tool for thinking and reflecting?
- ❏ communicate with others through writing?
- ❏ see themselves as writers in other areas of the curriculum?
- ❏ request feedback from others in planning and revising their writing?
- ❏ keep the audience in mind when writing?
- ❏ incorporate the computer into writing projects?
- ❏ keep a writing folder for their projects?
- ❏ publish a writing project each month?

Dolch Basic Sight Vocabulary

a	clean	green	many	run	together
about	cold	grow	may	said	too
after	come	had	me	saw	try
again	could	has	much	say	two
all	cut	have	must	see	under
always	did	he	my	seven	up
am	do	help	myself	shall	upon
an	does	her	never	she	us
and	done	here	new	show	use
any	don't	him	no	sing	very
are	down	his	not	sit	walk
around	draw	hold	now	six	want
as	drink	hot	of	sleep	warm
ask	eat	how	off	small	was
at	eight	hurt	old	so	wash
ate	every	I	on	some	we
away	fall	if	once	soon	well
be	far	in	one	start	went
because	fast	into	only	stop	were
been	find	is	open	take	what
before	first	it	or	tell	when
best	five	its	our	ten	where
better	fly	jump	out	thank	which
big	for	just	over	that	white
black	found	keep	own	the	who
blue	four	kind	pick	their	why
both	from	know	play	them	will
bring	full	laugh	please	then	wish
brown	funny	let	pretty	there	with
but	gave	light	pull	these	work
buy	get	like	put	they	would
by	give	little	ran	think	write
call	go	live	read	this	yellow
came	goes	long	red	those	yet
can	going	look	ride	three	you
carry	good	made	right	to	your
	got	make	round	today	

© 2004 *Literacy Techniques* by David Booth. Pembroke Publishers. Permission to copy for classroom use.

The First 200 Instant Words

The First Hundred Instant Words

Words 1–25	Words 26–50	Words 51–75	Words 76–100
the	or	will	number
of	one	up	no
and	had	other	way
a	by	about	could
to	word	out	people
in	but	many	my
is	not	then	than
you	what	them	first
that	all	these	water
it	were	so	been
he	we	some	call
was	when	her	who
for	your	would	oil
on	can	make	its
are	said	like	now
as	there	him	find
with	use	into	long
his	an	time	down
they	each	has	day
I	which	look	did
at	she	two	get
be	so	more	come
this	how	write	made
have	their	go	may
from	if	see	part

Words from 100–200

Words 101–125	Words 126–150	Words 151–175	Words 176–200
over	say	set	try
new	great	put	kind
sound	where	end	hand
take	help	does	picture
only	through	another	again
little	much	well	change
work	before	large	off
know	line	must	play
place	right	big	spell
year	too	even	air
live	mean	such	away
me	old	because	animal
back	any	turn	house
give	same	here	point
most	tell	why	page
very	boy	ask	letter
after	follow	went	mother
thing	came	men	answer
our	want	read	found
just	show	need	study
name	also	land	still
good	around	different	learn
sentence	form	home	should
man	three	us	Canada
think	small	move	work

Common suffixes: -s, -ing, -ed, -er; -ly, -est

Suggestions for Students on Keeping Reading Journals

- Make predictions about what may happen as the story progresses.
- Confirm your predictions, or refer to a previous entry you have made.
- Write about some surprises in the book, events and changes that you didn't anticipate, or puzzles that concern you.
- Transcribe a memorable quote or a special bit of dialogue from the book.
- Turn a powerful piece of prose from the book into a found poem.
- Discuss the big ideas in the book, the issues that take you "from the words" and "into the world".
- Discuss the genre of the book you are reading and be aware of the features of that particular type of writing.
- Discuss the cover illustration or other illustrations within the book, the layout of the book, or its structure.
- Connect the book to other books you have read by this author, such as a prequel or a sequel.
- Write about a special character you are drawn to or feel connected to, or discuss the changes in the character as the story developed.
- Notice the author's craft and connect it to your own efforts at becoming a writer.
- Comment on the author's apparent purpose for writing the book.
- Notice the writer's language, the use of special words or expressions, or memorable descriptions that stay with you.
- Comment on places in the book you have marked that in some way connect to your own life.
- Find connections to films and television programs, and to other books with similar themes.
- Give your own opinions about issues that have arisen from your reading the book.
- Examine the background and qualifications of the author.
- Question the accuracy of the author or challenge the author's ideas.
- Summarize the book or write a short précis about it.
- Discuss your difficulties and struggles as you read the book, or your reason for abandoning it.
- Discuss what you have learned from reading this book.

Graphic Organizer: Plot Organizer

Name: _____   Story Outline For _____

Author: _____   Publisher: _____   Date: _____

Setting/Main Characters

Story Theme

The Problem

Story Sequence

1.

2.

3.

Graphic Organizer: Mind Mapping Chart

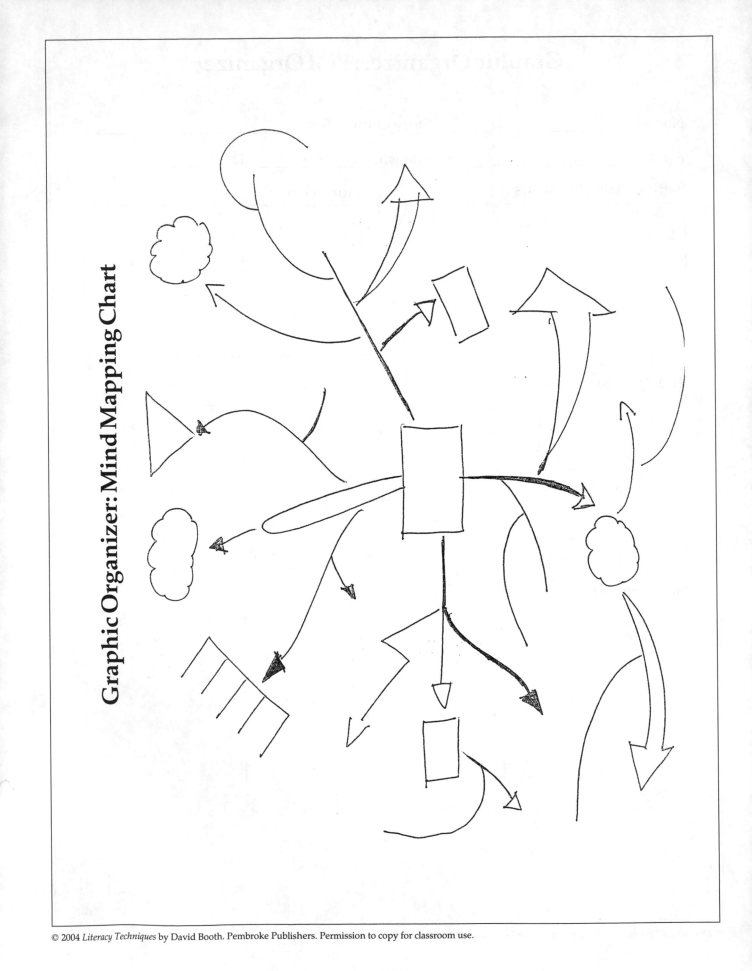

Graphic Organizer: Fact and Opinion

Fact	Opinion

Graphic Organizer: Prediction Chart

Page	What I Predict Will Happen	What Actually Happened

Graphic Organizer: 5-Ws

What–Who–Why–When–Where

What happened?
Who was there?
Why did it happen?
When did it happen?
Where did it happen?

Graphic Organizer: K–W–L Chart

K What (I) we know	W What (I) we want to find out	L What (I) we learned

Graphic Organizer: K–W–L Sequence Chart

TOPIC:_____

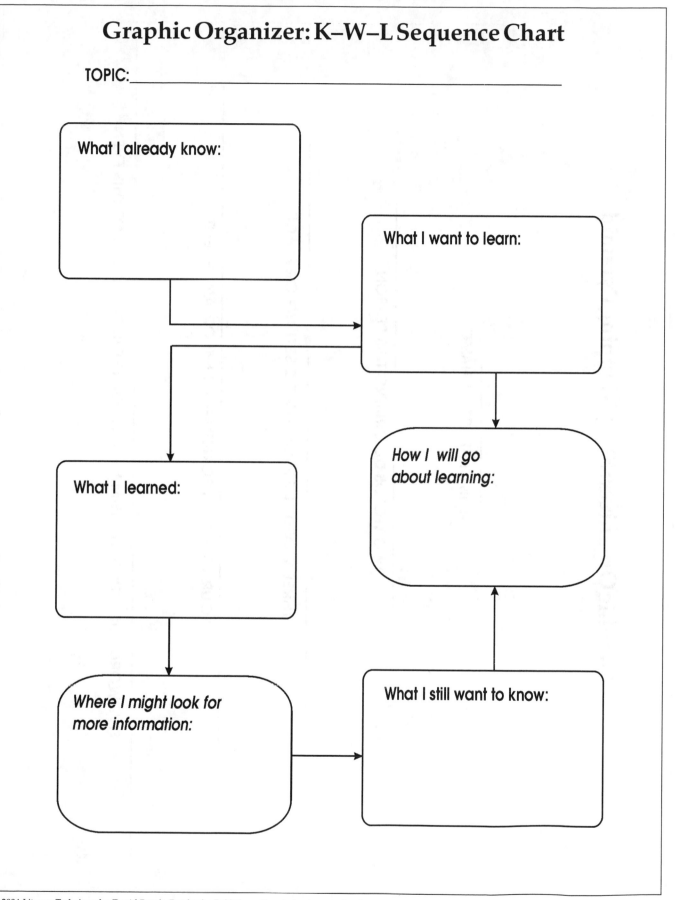

What I already know:

What I want to learn:

How I will go about learning:

What I learned:

Where I might look for more information:

What I still want to know:

Graphic Organizer: Story Mapping Pyramid

MAIN CHARACTER'S NAME

TWO WORDS DESCRIBING THIS PERSON

THREE WORDS DESCRIBING THE SETTING OR PLACE

FOUR WORDS DESCRIBING AN IMPORTANT EVENT

FIVE WORDS DESCRIBING THE MAIN IDEA OR THE IMPORTANCE OF THIS EVENT

An Editing Checklist

❏ Is your title engaging and representative of your project?

❏ Reread and look carefully at the overall theme or impression you want to give the reader.

❏ Should you add something—interesting vocabulary, an intriguing beginning or a stronger ending?

❏ Should you take something out—things that don't make sense, confusing words, boring words, words that are repeated?

❏ Should you move things around—rearrange paragraphs, words, or sentences to make more sense, be clearer, or sound better?

❏ Did you plan for your writing (researching, note taking, brainstorming, jotting down ideas, listing)?

❏ Are your ideas organized and easy to understand?

❏ Do your details strengthen your topic?

❏ Did you use examples to help the reader understand?

❏ Is your language and choice of words understood by your audience?

❏ Is your writing clear, concise, and to the point?

❏ Are sentences grammatically correct and do they make sense?

❏ Are words spelled correctly?

❏ Is the punctuation appropriate?

❏ Are words properly capitalized?

❏ If handwritten, is the writing neat and legible? If not, are the font and design appropriate?

❏ Are paragraphs properly formatted?

❏ Are quotations properly identified and formatted?

❏ Are headings and subheadings properly formatted?

❏ Are footnotes and/or endnotes properly identified and formatted?

❏ Is the bibliography properly formatted?

❏ Did you include all references?

❏ Would it help to illustrate your work with charts or diagrams?

❏ Would pictures or illustrations assist the reader?

❏ Do you have a special cover for your project?

❏ Have you submitted all the drafts?

❏ Is your writing folder complete?

Prompts to Use in Writing Conferences

What are you working on?

Do you want help with your writing?

I'm interested in this idea. Tell me more.

Why did you want to write about this topic?

Have you changed your mind while working on this topic?

What do you see in your mind's eye?

What do you want the reader to remember about your piece?

What is the most important point you are trying to make?

Do you think you have more than one topic here?

What is your favorite part?

Could you cut a piece out and use it in another project?

What about looking back at your idea web, or making a new one?

Do you need to find more information?

Where did this event happen?

What happened to cause this event?

Would a reader understand this part?

Can you expand this description?

Can you add your own reactions and feelings?

Why does this part matter?

Do you think a reader will care about this character?

Will a reader hear your own voice?

Read your lead aloud. Will it work for a reader?

How do you want the reader to feel at the end of the piece?

I am having trouble understanding this part. Can you help me to clarify it?

Have you thought of trying another pattern?

What about chunking the lines in your poem differently?

Do you think any illustrations might help?

Read this quotation aloud to me. Does it sound like real people talking?

Would adding some dialogue help in this section?

A Common Word Bank

the	I	you	and	of	said	brother	or
a	to	he	it	was	in	sister	Ms.
his	go	my	your	away	two	school	friend
that	we	would	time	man	or	still	next
she	one	me	from	old	head	much	open
for	then	will	good	by	door	keep	has
on	little	big	any	their	before	children	hard
they	down	mother	about	here	more	give	enough
but	do	went	Mr.	saw	eat	work	wait
had	can	are	father	call	oh	king	Mrs.
at	could	come	around	turn	again	first	morning
him	when	back	want	after	play	even	find
with	did	if	don't	well	who	cry	only
up	what	now	how	think	been	try	us
all	thing	other	know	ran	may	new	three
look	so	long	right	let	stop	must	our
is	see	no	put	help	odd	grand	found
her	not	came	too	side	never	start	why
there	were	ask	got	house	eye	soon	girl
some	get	day	take	home	took	made	place
out	them	very	where	thought	people	run	under
as	like	boy	every	make	say	hand	while
be	just	an	dog	walk	tree	began	told
have	this	over	way	water	tell	gave	than

Appendix 2: Book Lists

Grades 1, 2, 3

Grades 4, 5, 6

Grades 7, 8

Grades 1, 2, 3

Read Aloud

Allen, Susan and Jane Lindaman. *Read Anything Good Lately?* Brookfield, CT: The Millbrook Press.

Bogart, Jo Ellen. *Jeremiah Learns to Read.* New York, NY: Scholastic.

Browne, Anthony. *Into the Forest.* Cambridge, MA: Candlewick Press.

Burningham, John. *Would You Rather...?* New York, NY: SeaStar Books. (Also: *Cloudland; Mr. Gumpy's Outing; Mr. Gumpy's Motor Car; Where's Julius?*)

Cronin, Doreen. *Click, Clack, Moo: Cows that Type.* (Also: *Diary of a Worm; Giggle, Giggle Quack; Duck for President.*)

Falconer, Ian. *Olivia.* New York, NY: Atheneum. (Also: *Olivia Goes to the Circus; Olivia and the Missing Toy*).

Fox, Mem. *Wilfred Gordon McDonald Partridge.* Illustrated by Julie Vivas. La Jolla, CA: Kane Miller. (Also: *Koala Lou.*)

Henkes, Kevin. *Chrysanthemum.* New York, NY: Greenwillow. (Also: *Lily's Purple Plastic Purse, Owen, Wemberly Worries.*)

Lee, Chinlun. *The Very Kind Rich Lady and Her One Hundred Dogs.* Cambridge, MA: Candlewick Press.

Lottridge, Celia. *The Name of the Tree.* Illustrated by Ian Wallace. Toronto, ON: Douglas and McIntyre.

Martin, Bill Jr. and Jon Archambault. *Chicka Chicka Boom Boom.* Illustrated by Lois Ehlert. New York, NY: Henry Holt. (Also: *Chicka, Chicka 1, 2, 3.*)

Prelutsky, Jack, ed. *Read-Aloud Rhymes for the Very Young.* New York, NY: Alfred A. Knopf.

Scieszka, Jon. *The True Story of the Three Little Pigs.* Illustrated by Lane Smith. New York, NY: Viking.

Sendak, Maurice. *Where the Wild Things Are.* New York, NY: HarperCollins.

Yolen, Jane. *Owl Moon.* New York, NY: Philomel.

Shared Reading

Baker, Keith. *Who is the Beast?* San Diego, CA: Harcourt.

Denton, Kady MacDonald. *A Child's Treasury of Nursery Rhymes.* Toronto, ON: Kids Can Press.

Feiffer, Jules. *Bark, George!* New York, NY: HarperCollins.

Hall, Donald. (1994). *I am the Dog/I am the Cat.* New York, NY: Dial Books.

Heidbreder, Robert. *See Saw Saskatchewan.* (Also: *Don't Eat Spiders; Eenie Meenie Manitoba.*)

Hoberman, Mary Ann. *You Read To Me, I'll Read to You: Very short stories to read together.* New York, NY: Philomel. (Also: *You Read to Me, I'll Read to You: Very short fairy tales to read together.*)

Hort, Lenny. *The Seals on the Bus.* Illustrated by G. Brian Karas. New York, NY: Henry Holt and Company.

Jenkins, Steve and Robin Page. *What Do You Do With A Tail Like This?* Boston, MA: Houghton Mifflin. (Also: *Actual Size.*)

Lee, Dennis. *Bubblegum Delicious.* Toronto, ON: Key Porter Books. (Also: *Alligator Pie; Garbage Delight; The Ice Cream Store; Jelly Belly.*)

Lesynski, Loris. *Nothing Beats a Pizza.* Toronto, ON: Annick Press. (Also: *Cabbagehead; Dirty Dog Boogie.*)

Martin, Bill Jr. and Eric Carle. *Brown Bear, Brown Bear, What do you see?.* New York, NY: Henry Holt. (Also: *Polar Bear, Polar Bear, What do you hear?: Panda Bear, Panda Bear, Where do you hide?*)

Raschka, Chris. *Yo! Yes?* New York, NY: Orchard.

Rosen, Michael. *We're Going on a Bear Hunt.* Illustrated by Helen Oxenbury. London, UK: Walker Books.

Taback, Simms. *Joseph Had a Little Overcoat.* New York, NY: Aladdin Classics.

Williams, Linda. *The Little Old Lady Who Was Not Afraid of Anything.* New York, NY: HarperCollins.

Emergent Readers

Carle, Eric. *"Slowly, Slowly, Slowly", Said the Sloth.* New York, NY: Philomel Books. (Also: *Do You Want to Be My Friend?; The Grouch Ladybug; Mister Seahorse; The Very Quiet Cricket; The Very Hungry Caterpillar.*)

Catalonotto, Peter. *Matthew ABC.* New York, NY: Atheneum.

Cousins, Lucy. *Jazzy in the Jungle.* Cambridge, MA: Candlewick Press.

Cuyler, Margery. *Roadsigns.* Delray Beach, FLA: Winslow Press.

Ehlert, Lois. *In My World*. San Diego, CA: Harcourt. (Also: *Fish Eyes; Growing Vegetable Soup; Hands; Planting a Rainbow; Red Leaf, Yellow Leaf; Snowballs, Waiting for Wings*.)

Joyce. William. *George Shrinks*. New York, NY: HarperCollins.

Marzollo, Jean. *I Spy: A picture book of riddles* (Series.) Photographs by Walter Wick. New York, NY: Scholastic.

Most, Bernard. *There's An Ant In Anthony*. New York, NY: Mulberry Books.

Parr, Todd. *The Peace Book*. New York, NY: Little Brown and Company. (Also: *The Best Friends Book; The Feelings Book; It's OK To Be Different*.)

Seuss, Dr. *One Fish Two Fish Red Fish Blue Fish*. New York, NY: Random House. (Also: *The Cat in the Hat; Green Eggs and Ham; Horton Hatches the Egg; The 500 Hats of Bartholomew Cubbins*.)

Shannon, David. *No, David!* New York, NY: Scholastic, Inc. (Sequels: *David Gets in Trouble; David Goes to School*.)

Thomas, Shelley Moore. *Somewhere Today*. New York, NY: Albert Whitman and Company.

Wood, Audrey. *Silly Sally*. San Diego, CA: Harcourt.

Yolen, Jane. *Off We Go!* New York, NY: Little Brown and Company.

Young, Ed. *Seven Blind Mice*. New York, NY: Philomel.

Developing Readers

Adler, David. *Cam Jansen* (Series.) New York, NY: Puffin.

Bourgeois, Paulette. *Franklin* (Series). Illustrated by Brenda Clark. Toronto, ON: Kids Can Press.

Brown, Anthony. *Willy the Champ* (Series). New York, NY: Alfred A. Knopf.

Brown, Mark. *Arthur* (Series). New York, NY: Little Brown.

Gilman, Phoebe. *Something from Nothing*. Richmond Hill, ON: North Winds. (Also: *Jillian Jiggs* Series.)

Keats, Ezra Jack. *The Snowy Day*. New York, NY: Penguin. (Also: *Hi, Cat!; Pet Show; The Trip; Whistle for Willie*.)

Lionni, Leo. *Frederick*. New York, NY: Pantheon. (Also: *Alexander and the Wind-up Mouse; Fish is Fish; Swimmy; Tilly and the Wall*.)

Lobel, Arnold. *Days with Frog and Toad* (Series). New York, NY: HarperCollins. (Also: *Mouse Soup; Mouse Tales, Owl at Home; Uncle Elephant*.)

Numeroff, Laura. *If You Give a Moose a Muffin* (Series). Illustrated by Felicia Bond. New York, NY: HarperCollins.

Parish, Peggy. *Amelia Bedelia* (Series). New York, NY: HarperCollins.

Rylant, Cynthia. *Henry and Mudge* (Series). New York, NY: Simon & Schuster.

Sachar, Louis. *Marvin Redpost* (Series). New York, NY: Random House.

Sharmat, Marjorie Weinman. *Nate the Great* (Series). New York, NY: Random House.

Wormell, Chris. *Two Frogs*. London, UK: Jonothan Cape.

Zion, Gene. *Harry the Dirty Dog* (Series). Ilustrated by Margaret B. Graham. New York, NY: Harper & Row.

Independent Readers

Allen, Judy. *Tiger*. Cambridge, MA: Candlewick Press. (Also: *Elephant; Panda; Seal; Whale*.)

Cannon, Janell. *Stellaluna*. San Diego, CA: Harcourt Brace. (Also: *Crickwing; Verdi*)

Clements, Andrew. *Jake Drake* (Series.) New York, NY: Aladdin.

Cole, Joanna. *The Magic School Bus* (Series). New York, NY: Scholastic.

Gay, Marie-Louise. *Stella, Princess of the Sky* (Series). Toronto, ON: Groundwood. (Also: *Good Morning, Sam; Good Night Sam*.)

Giff, Patricia Reilly. *The Kids of The Polk Street School* (Series). New York, NY: Dell Yearling.

Jocelyn, Marthe. *Hannah's Collections*. New York, NY: Dutton Children's Books. (Also: *Hannah and the Seven Dresses*)

Marshall, James. *George and Martha* (Series). Boston, MA: Houghton Mifflin.

McDonald, Megan. *Judy Moody* (Series). Cambridge, MA: Candlewick Press.

King-Smith, Dick. *The Sheep Pig (Babe)*. London, UK: Victor Gollancz. (Also: *Daggie Dogfoot; The Fox Busters; Harry's Mad; Pets for Keeps*.)

MacLachlan, Patricia. *Sarah Plain and Tall*. New York, NY: Harper Row. (Sequels: *Skylark; Caleb's Song*.)

Park, Barbara. *Junie B. Jones* (Series). New York, NY: Random House.

Pilkey, Dav. *The Dumb Bunnies* (Series). New York, NY: HarperCollins.

Silverstein, Shel. *The Giving Tree*. New York, NY: HarperCollins.

Steig, William. *Doctor De Soto*. New York, NY: Farrar, Straus & Giroux. (Also: *Gorky Rising; Pete's a Pizza; Rotten Island, Solomon and the Rusty Nai; Sylvester and the Magic Pebble: When Everybody Wore a Hat*.)

Grades 4, 5, 6

Read Aloud

Avi. *The End of the Beginning*. San Diego, CA: Harcourt.

Babbitt, Natalie. *Tuck Everlasting*. New York, NY: Bantam.

Barton, Bob. *The Bear Says North: Tales from Northern Lands*. Illustrated by Jirina Marton. Toronto, ON: Groundwood.

Booth, David. *The Dust Bowl*. Toronto, ON: Kids Can Press.

Crossley-Holland, Kevin. *Enchantment: Fairy tales, ghost stories and tales of wonder*. London, UK: Orion Books.

DiCamillo, Kate. *The Tale of Despereaux*. Cambridge, MA: Candlewick Press.

Gardiner, John Reynolds. *Stone Fox*. New York, NY: HarperCollins.

Levine, Karen. *Hana's Suitcase*. Toronto, ON: Second Story Press.

Maguire, Gregory. *Leaping Beauty: And other animal fairy tales*. New York, NY: HarperCollins.

McKee, David. *The Conquerors*. London, UK: Andersen Press.

Polacco, Patricia. *Thank You, Mr. Falker*. New York, NY: Philomel. (Also: *Chicken Sunday, The Keeping Quilt, Mr. Lincoln's Way*.)

Rappaport, Doreen. *Martin's Big Words*. New York, NY: Hyperion.

Steig, William. *Abel's Island*. New York, NY: Bantam.

Wallace, Ian. (1999). *Boy of the Deeps*. Toronto, ON: Groundwood.

Wild, Margaret. *Fox*. Illustrated by Ron Brooks. La Jolla, CA: Kane Miller.

Ye Ting-xing. *White Lily*. Toronto, ON: Doubleday.

Shared Reading

Bennett, Jill, ed. *Peace Begins With Me*. Oxford, UK: Oxford University Press.

Booth, David. *Til All the Stars Have Fallen*. Toronto, ON: Kids Can Press.

Bouchard, David. *The Song Within My Heart*. Art by Allen Sapp. Vancouver, BC: Raincoast Books. (Also: *If You're Not from the Prairie; The Elders Are Watching*)

Ewald, Wendy. *The Best Part of Me*. New York, NY: Little Brown and Company.

Fitch, Sheree. *There Were Monkeys in the Kitchen*. Illustrated by Mark Mongeau. Toronto, ON: Doubleday.

Florian, Douglas. *Laugh-eteria*. San Diego, CA: Harcourt. (Also: *Bing, Bang Bong*.)

Florian, Douglas. *Insectlopedia*. San Diego, CA: Harcourt. (Also: *Beast Feast; Bow Wow Meow Meow; In the Swim; On the Wing*)

Frost, Helen. *Spinning Through the Universe: A novel in poems from Room 214*. New York, NY: Farrar Straus & Giroux.

Gonsalves, Ron. *Imagine A Night*. New York, NY: Simon & Schuster.

Moss, Marissa. *Amelia's Notebook* (Series). Berkeley, CA: Tricycle Press.

Prelutsky, Jack. *It's Raining Pigs and Noodles*. New York, NY: HarperCollins. (Also: *The New Kid on the Block; Something Big Has Been Here; A Pizza the Size of the Sun*.)

Scieszka, Jon. *Science Verse*. Illustrated by Lane Smith. New York, NY: Viking. (Also: *Squids Will Be Squids*.)

Seskin, Steve and Alan Shamblin. *Don't Laugh At Me*. Berkeley, CA: Tricycle Press.

Tang, Greg. *The Grapes of Math* (Series). New York, NY: Scholastic.

Ulmer, Mike. *M is for Maple*. Toronto, ON: Sleeping Bear Press. (Also: *Z is for Zamboni*.)

Struggling Readers

Blume, Judy. *Tales of a Fourth Grade Nothing* (Series). New York, NY: Dell.

Dadey, Debbie and Marcia Thornton Jones. *The Adventures of the Bailey School Kids* (Series). New York, NY: Scholastic.

Delton, Judy. *Pee Wee Scouts* (Series). New York, NY: Dell.

Doyle, Roddy. *The Giggler Treatment*. New York, NY: Scholastic. (Also: *The Meanwhile Adventures*.)

Griffiths, Andy. *Just Annoying*. New York, NY: Scholastic. (Also: *Just Joking; Just Stupid; Just Wacky*.)

Howe, James and Deborah. *Bunnicula* (Series). New York, NY: Puffin.

Korman, Gordon. *Island* (Trilogy). New York, NY: Scholastic. (Also: *The Dive Trilogy; The Everest Trilogy.*)

Osborne, Mary Pope. *The Magic Tree House* (Series). New York, NY: Harper and Row.

Pilkey, Dav. *The Adventures of Captain Underpants* (Series). New York, NY: Scholastic.

Sachar, Louis. *Sideways Stories from a Wayside School* (Series). New York, NY: Avon Books.

Scieszka, Jon. *The Time Warp Trio* (Series). New York, NY: Viking.

Snicket, Lemony. *A Series of Unfortunate Events* (Series). New York, NY: HarperCollins.

Stine, R.L. *Beware!: R.L. Stine picks his favorite scary stories.* New York NY: HarperCollins.

Stilton, Geronimo. *The Curse of the Cheese Pyramid* (Series). New York, NY: Scholastic.

Van Allsburg, Chris. *Jumanji.* Boston: MA: Houghton Mifflin. (Also: *The Garden of Abdul Gasazi; They Mysteries of Harris Burdick; The Polar Express; The Stranger; Two Bad Ants; The Wretched Stone.*)

Developing Readers

Avi. *Poppy* (Series). New York, NY: Avon Books. (Also: *Crispin; Perloo The Bold.*)

Cleary, Beverly. *Dear Mr. Henshaw.* New York, NY: Morrow. (Sequel: *Strider.*)

Cleary, Beverly. *The Mouse and the Motorcycle* (Trilogy). New York, NY: Morrow.

Clements, Andrew. *The Jacket.* New York, NY: Simon & Schuster. (Also: *Frindle; The Landry News: The Janitor's Boy; The School Story*).

Creech, Sharon. *Love That Dog.* New York, NY: HarperCollins.

Curtis, Christopher Paul. *The Watsons Go To Birmingham – 1963.* New York, NY: Delacorte Press. (Also: *Bucking the Sarge; Bud, Not Buddy.*)

Dahl, Roald. *James and the Giant Peach.* New York, NY: Alfred A. Knopf. (Also: *Charlie and the Chocolate Factory; Matilda; The Twits; The Witches.*)

Ellis, Deborah. *The Breadwinner* (Trilogy). Toronto, ON: Douglas and McIntyre. (Also: *Parvana's Journey; Mud City.*)

Gantos, Jack. *Joey Pigza Swallowed the Key.* New York, NY: HarperCollins. (Sequels: *Joey Pigza Loses Control; What Would Joey Do?*)

Hiaasen, Carl. *Hoot.* New York, NY: Alfred A. Knopf.

Holt, Kimberly Willis. *When Zachary Beaver Came to Town.* New York, NY: Henry Holt and Company.

Huser, Glen. *Stitches.* Toronto, ON: Douglas and McIntyre.

Korman, Gordon. *This Can't be Happening at MacDonald Hall.* Toronto, ON: Scholastic. (Also: *Beware the Fish; Bruno and Boots; The Chicken Doesn't Skate; Fifth Grade Radio; Why did the Underwear Cross the Road?; The Zucchini Warriors.*)

Levine, Gail Carson. *Ella Enchanted.* New York, NY: HarperCollins.

Lottridge, Celia Barker. *Ticket to Curlew.* Toronto, ON: Groundwood. (Sequel: *Wings to Fly.*)

Lowry, Lois. *Number the Stars.* New York, NY: Bantam Doubleday.

Mazer, Anne. *The Amazing Days of Abby Hayes* (Series). New York, NY: Scholastic.

Naylor, Phyllis Reynolds. *Shiloh.* New York, NY: Bantam Doubleday. (Sequels: *Shiloh Season; Saving Shiloh.*)

Park, Barbara. *The Graduation of Jake Moon.* New York, NY: Aladdin.

Paterson, Katherine. *Bridge to Terabithia.* New York, NY: Harper Trophy. (Also: *The Great Gilly Hopkins, Field of Dogs*)

Richler, Mordecai. *Jacob Two-Two Meets the Hooded Fang* (Trilogy). New York, NY: Alfred A. Knopf.

Scrimger, Richard. *The Nose from Jupiter.* Toronto, ON: Tundra Books. (Also: *A Nose for Adventure; Noses are Red.*)

Seidler, Tor. *Mean Margaret.* New York, NY: HarperCollins.

Van Draanen, Wendelin. *Shredderman: Secret Identity.* New York, NY: Alfred A. Knopf.

Walters, Eric. *Run.* Toronto, ON: Penguin Books. (Also: *Hoop Crazy; The Money Pit Mystery; Tiger Town; Trapped in Ice.*)

Independent Readers

Alexander, Lloyd. *The Book of Three* (Series). New York, NY: Dell.

Colfer, Eoin. *Artimus Fowl.* New York, NY: Puffin. (Sequel: *Artemis Fowl: The Arctic Incident.*)

Funke, Cornelia. *The Thief Lord.* New York, NY: Scholastic. (Also: *Dragon Rider; Inkheart.*)

Gaiman, Neil. *Coraline.* New York, NY: HarperCollins.

Hesse, Karen. *The Music of Dolphins.* New York, NY: Scholastic.

Hoeye, Michael. *Time Stops for No Mouse*. Portland, OR: Terfle Books. (Sequel: *The Sands of Time*.)

Jacques, Brian. *Redwall* (Series). London, UK: Random House.

L'Engle, Madeline. *A Wrinkle in Time* (Trilogy). New York, NY: Farrar, Straus & Giroux.

Little, Jean. *Mama's Going To Buy You A Mockingbird*. Toronto, ON: Penguin.

Oppel, Kenneth. *Silverwing* (Trilogy). Toronto, ON: HarperCollins.

Paolini, Christopher. *Eragon*. New York, NY: Alfred A. Knopf

Paulsen, Gary. *Hatchet*. New York, NY: Puffin. (Also: *Brian's Hunt; Brian's Return; Brian's Winter; Guts*.)

Rowling, J.K. *Harry Potter* (Series). Vancouver, BC: Raincoast.

Sachar, Louis. *Holes*. New York, NY: Farrar, Straus & Giroux.

Spinelli, Jerry. *Wringer*. New York, NY: HarperCollins. (Also: *Loser, Maniac Magee, Stargirl*.)

Grades 7, 8

Read Aloud

Almond, David. *Skellig*. London, UK: Hodder Children's Books.

Armstrong, Jennifer. *Shattered: Stories of Children and War*. New York, NY: Alfred A. Knopf.

Bunting, Eve. *Riding the Tiger*. New York, NY: Clarion Books. (Also: *Gleam and Glow; Smoky Night*.)

Cooper, Susan. *The Selkie Girl*. Illustrated by Warwick Hutton. New York, NY: Margaret K McElderry Books.

Howe, James. *Thirteen*. New York, NY: Atheneum.

Muth, Jon J. *The Three Questions*. New York, NY: Scholastic.

Spinelli, Jerry. *Milkweed*. New York, NY: Alfred A. Knopf.

Trelease, Jim, ed. *Read All About It: Great read-aloud stories, poems, and newspaper pieces for preteens and teens*. New York, NY: Penguin Books.

Yee, Paul. *Tales from Gold Mountain*. Toronto, ON: Groundwood. (Also: *Dead Man's Gold and other stories; Ghost Train*.)

Yolen, Jane. *Here There Be Ghosts*. San Diego, CA: Harcourt. (Also: *Here There Be Witches: Here There Be Dragons; Here There Be Unicorns; Here There Be Angels*.)

Shared Reading

Appelt, Kathi. *Poems from Homeroom*. New York, NY: Henry Holt and Company.

Fleischman, Paul. *Seedfolks*. New York, NY: HarperCollins.

Gaiman, Neil. *The Wolves in the Walls*. New York, NY: HarperCollins.

Hesse, Karen. *Out of the Dust*. New York, NY: Aladdin.

Major, Kevin. *Ann and Seamus*. Toronto, ON: Groundwood.

Marsden, John. *Prayer for the Twenty-first Century*. New York, NY: Star Bright Books.

Nye, Noami Shihab. *This Same Sky: A collection of poems from around the world*. New York, NY: Four Winds Press.

Smith Jr., Charles R. *Rimshots: Basketball Pix, Rolls and Rhythms*. New York, NY: Dutton Children's Books.

Weatherford, Carole Boston. *Remember the Bridge: Poems of a people*. New York, NY: Philomel Books.

Struggling Readers

Applegate, K.A. *Animorphs* (Series). New York, NY: Scholastic.

Brashare, Ann. *The Sisterhood of the Traveling Pants*. New York, NY: Dell Laurel. (Also: *The Secret Summer of the Sisterhood; The Second Summer of the Traveling Pants*.)

Cabot, Meg. *The Princess Diaries* (Series). New York, NY: HarperCollins.

Crutcher, Chris. *Athletic Shorts*. New York, NY: Greenwillow. (Also: *The Crazy Horse Electric Game; Running Loose; Stotan*.)

Griffiths, Andy. *The Day My Butt Went Psycho*. New York, NY: Scholastic. (Sequel: *Zombie Butts from Uranus*).

Hinton, S.E. *The Outsiders*. New York, NY: Dell. (Also: *Rumble Fish; Tex; That Was Then/This is Now*.)

Korman, Gordon. *No More Dead Dogs*. New York, NY: Hyperion. (Also: *Son of the Mob; Son of the Mob 2*)

Schwartz, Alvin. *Scary Stories to Tell in the Dark* (Series). New York, NY: HarperCollins.

Von Ziegesa, Cecily. *The Gossip Girl* (Series). New York, NY: Little Brown and Company.

Walters, Eric. *STARS*. Toronto, ON: Penguin Books. (Also: *Diamonds in the Rough: The Bully Boys; Camp X; Visions*)

Developing Readers

Anderson, Laurie Halse. *Speak*. New York, NY: Farrar, Straus & Giroux.

Avi. *Nothing But the Truth*. New York, NY: Avon.

Bloor, Edward. *Tangerine*. New York, NY: Scholastic.

Creech, Sharon. (2004). *Heartbeat*. New York, NY: HarperCollins. (Also: *Walk Two Moons*.)

Doyle, Bryan. *Up to Low*. Toronto, ON: Douglas and McIntyre. (Also: *Angel Square; Hey Dad: Mary Ann Alice; Spuds Sweetgrass*.)

Fine, Anne. *Flour Babies*. London, UK: Puffin Books.

Gardner, Graham. *Inventing Elliot*. New York, NY: Dial Books.

George, Jean Craighead. *Julie of the Wolves*. New York, NY: HarperCollins.

Holman, Felice. *Slake's Limbo*. New York, NY: Aladdin.

Konigsburg, E.L. *Silent to the Bone*. New York, NY: Atheneum.

Lowry, Lois. *The Giver*. Boston, MA: Houghton Mifflin. (Also: *Gathering Blue; Messenger*.)

Major, Kevin. *Hold Fast*. New York, NY: Dell. (Also: *Dear Bruce Springsteen; Far From Shore; No Man's Land*.)

Oppel, Kenneth. *Airborn*. New York, NY: HarperCollins.

Pierce, Tamora. *Protector of the Small Quartet* (Series). New York, NY: Random House.

Singer, Nicky. *Feather Boy*. London, UK: HarperCollins.

Tashijan, Janet. *The Gospel According to Larry*. New York, NY: Henry Holt and Company.

Taylor, Mildred D. *Roll of Thunder Hear My Cry*. New York, NY: Puffin.

Van Drannen, Wendelin. *Flipped*. New York, NY: Alfred A. Knopf.

Whelan, Gloria. *Homeless Bird*. New York, NY: HarperCollins.

Wynne-Jones, Tim. *A Thief in the House of Memory*. Toronto, ON: Groundwood. (Also: *The Maestro; Stephen Fair; The Boy in the Burning House*.)

Independent Readers

Cooper, Susan. *The Dark is Rising* (Series). London, UK: Puffin.

Cormier, Robert. *The Rag and Bone Shop*. New York, NY: Delacorte Press. (Also: *After the First Death; The Bumblebee Summer; Frenchtown Summer; I Am the Cheese*.)

Crossley-Holland, Kevin. *Arthur: The Seeing Stone* (Trilogy). London, UK: Orion.

LeGuin, Ursula. *A Wizard of Earthsea* (Trilogy). New York, NY: Bantam.

Myers, Walter Dean. *Monster*. New York, NY: Scholastic. (Also: *The Beast; Shooter; Scorpions; Slam!*)

Nix, Garth. *Sabriel*. New York, NY: HarperCollins. (Sequel: *Lirael*.)

Paulsen, Gary. *The Rifle*. New York, NY: Laurel-Leaf. (Also: *The Beet Fields; The Car; The Island; Dancing Carl; Dogsong; Soldier's Heart; Tracker*.)

Pullman, Philip. *The Golden Compass* (Trilogy). New York, NY: Ballantine.

Slade, Arthur. *Dust*. Toronto, ON: HarperCollins.

Townsend. Sue. *The Secret Diary of Adrian Mole Age 13 ¾* (Trilogy). London, UK: Methuen.

Bibliography

Allen, Janet (2002). *On the same page: Shared reding beyond the primary grades.* Portland, ME: Stenhouse Publishers; Markham, ON: Pembroke Publishers.

Allen, Janet (2000). *Yellow Brick Roads: Shared and Guided Paths to Independent Reading 4–12.* Portland, ME: Stenhouse Publishers; Markham, ON: Pembroke Publishers.

Atwell, Nancie (1998). *In the Middle: New understandings about reading, writing, reading and learning.* 2nd ed. Portsmouth, NH: Heinemann.

Beers, Kylene (2003). *When Kids Can't Read: What Teachers Can Do.* York, ME: Stenhouse Publishers; Markham, ON: Pembroke Publishers.

Booth, David (2002). *Even Hockey Players Read: Boys, literacy and learning.* Markham, ON: Pembroke Publishers.

Booth, David (2001). *Reading and Writing in the Middle Years.* Markham, ON: Pembroke Publishers.

Booth, David and Bob Barton (2000). *Story Works.* Markham, ON: Pembroke Publishers.

Booth, David, Joan Green, and Jack Booth (2004). *I Want to Read!: Reading, writing and really learning.* Oakville, ON: Rubicon Publishing Inc; Toronto, ON: Harcourt Canada.

Brand, Max (2004). *Word Savvy: Integrated vocabulary, spelling and word study, Grades 3–6.* Portland, ME: Stenhouse Publishers; Markham, ON: Pembroke Publishers.

Calkins, Lucy McCormick (1991). *Living Between the Lines.* Portsmouth, NH: Heinemann.

Calkins, Lucy McCormick (2000). *The Art of Teaching Reading.* Portsmouth, NH: Heinemann.

Calkins, Lucy and Pat Bleichman (2003). *The Craft of Revision.* Portsmouth, NH: Heinemann.

Calkins, Lucy McCormick and Janet Angelillo (2002). *A Fresh Approach to Teaching Punctuation: Helping young writers use conventions with precision and purpose.* New York, NY: Scholastic.

Coelho, Elizabeth (2003). *Adding English: A guide to teaching in multilingual classrooms.* Portsmouth, NH: Heinemann; Toronto, ON: Pippin Publishers.

Daniels, Harvey (1994/ 2002). *Literature Circles: Voice and Choice in the Student-Centred Classroom.* Portland, ME: Stenhouse Publishers; Markham, ON: Pembroke Publishers.

Fletcher, Ralph and JoAnn Portalupi (1998). *Craft Lessons: Teaching writing K–8.* Portland, ME: Stenhouse Publishers; Markham, ON: Pembroke Publishers. (Also: *Nonfiction Craft Lessons.*)

Fountas, Irene C., and Gay Su Pinell (1994). *Guided Reading: Good first teaching for all children.* Portsmouth, NH: Heinemann. (Also: *Guided Reading 4–6.*)

Harvey, Stephanie and Anne Goudvi (2000). *Strategies That Work: Teaching comprehension to enhance understanding.* Portland, ME: Stenhouse Publishers; Markham, ON: Pembroke Publishers.

Harwayne, Shelley (2001). *Writing Through Childhood: Rethinking process and product.* Portsmouth, NH: Heinemann.

Hindley, Joanne (1996). *In the Company of Children.* Portland, ME: Stenhouse Publishers; Markham, ON: Pembroke Publishers.

Keene, Ellin Oliver and Susan Zimmerman (1997). *Mosaic of Thought: Teaching comprehension in a reader's workshop.* Portsmouth, NH: Heinemann.

Lundy, Kathleen Gould (2004). *What Do I Do About the Kid Who…50 Ways to turn teaching into learning.* Markham, ON: Pembroke Publishers.

Marshall, Jodi Crum (2002). *Are They Really Reading: Expanding SSR in the middle grades.* York, ME: Stenhouse Publishers; Markham, ON: Pembroke Publishers.

Marten, Cindy (2003). *Word Crafting: Teaching spelling grades K–6.* Portsmouth, NH: Heinemann.

Miller, Debbie (2002). *Reading With Meaning: Teaching comprehension in the Primary Grades.* Portland, ME: Stenhouse Publishers; Markham, ON: Pembroke Publishers.

Peterson, Shelley (2003). *Guided Writing Instruction: Strategies to help students become better writers.* Winnipeg, MB: Portage & Main Press.

Rog, Lori Jamison (2003). *Guided Reading Basics: Organizing, managing, and implementing a balanced literacy program in K–3.* Markham, ON: Pembroke Publishers.

Routman, Regie (2002). *Reading Essentials: The specifics you need to teach reading well.* Portsmouth, NH: Heinemann.

Schwartz, Susan and Mindy Pollishuke (2002). *Creating the Dynamic Classroom: A handbook for teachers*. Toronto, ON: Pearson Publishing.

Stead, Tony (2001). *Is That a Fact?: Teaching nonfiction writing K–3*. Portland, ME: Stenhouse Publishers.

Swartz, Larry (2002). *The New Dramathemes*. Toronto, ON: Pembroke Publishers.

Taberski, Sharon (2000). *On Solid Ground: Strategies for teaching reading K–3*. Portsmouth, NH: Heinemann.

Tovani, Cris (2004). *Do I Really Have to Teach Reading?: Content comprehension Grades 6–12*. Portland, ME: Stenhouse Publishers; Markham, ON: Pembroke Publishers.

Wells, Jan and Janine Reid (2004). *Writing Anchors*. Markham, ON: Pembroke Publishers.

Index

142